OLD ACT NEVER DIE...

THEY SIMPLY LOSE THE PLOT

A Farce In Two Acts

Lynn Brittney

Published by Playstage
United Kingdom.

An imprint of Write Publications Ltd

www.playsforadults.com

Designed by Kate Lowe, Greensands Graphics
Printed by Creeds Ltd, Bridport, Dorset

Note to producers about staging "Old Actors Never Die..."

This is a farce and therefore a good pace is important as the play progresses. There should be no significant pauses between characters exiting the stage and another character entering.

ANN is a brisk woman, slightly harassed and slightly unsure of all the "actor-types" in her charge.

WALTER should never be played camp. Although he is gay, he has spent his entire life playing military roles and is always very butch, except at the beginning of the play when he is chanting the rhyme with the three women.

The three MRS SULLIVANs are all slightly eccentric and fun-loving. PHYL is the leader of the trio – the most sensible and quick-witted. JULES is a bit flirty and stuck in a seventies'time-warp. BECCA is a bit scatty and vague.

MARCIA is a starstruck chatterbox, who is always smiling.

DANNY STILLER – there must be a marked contrast between Danny the insecure, grieving, self-pitying widower and Danny the all-powerful Master of The Universe.

EDMUND is confident and sexy but vague, as though he can hardly remember people's names and has been looked after all his life. His overwhelming confidence should never leave him – even when he is threatened with death and mutilation by the Russian gangster.

MIKE MOLINSKY – must display the Russian ability to change moods in a flash. He is definitely unhinged but, usually, is very controlled and used to being in command of everyone.

DMITRI – totally unsmiling and conveys menace. Wears dark glasses and stands like a bouncer.

IRINA – another unsmiling character but always glamorous, in a hard way.

CAST LIST

ANN THOMPSON	the administrator of the Mount Home for Retired Theatricals – age – in her 40's
WALTER NEVILLE	retired bit-part actor. Military bearing, very brisk. Age - 70+
PHYLLIDA SULLIVAN	retired actress, first ex-wife of Edmund Sullivan – aged 70+- known as Phyl. Very clever and the leader of the women.
JULES SULLIVAN	retired actress, second ex-wife of Edmund Sullivan. Aged 60+. A bit bohemian and occasionally flirtatious. Known as Jules.
REBECCA SULLIVAN	retired actress, third ex-wife of Edmund Sullivan. Aged 60+. Slightly scatty. Known as Becca.
MARCIA	the housekeeper. Very chatty. Obsessed with actors. Age 30-40
DANNY STILLER	a wealthy retired actor. Very neurotic and timid. Used to be very confident – even arrogant. Aged 60+
MIKE MOLINSKY	a vicious, unhinged, but comical Russian gangster. Sharp dresser. Carries a scalpel around with him. Aged 30+
EDMUND SULLIVAN	still appearing in major movies. Very confident and charming and has a long history of seduction and adultery. Age 70.
DMITRI	non-speaking part. Large, menacing bodyguard. Any age.
IRINA	glamorous but menacing Russian woman of uncertain age.

6 females and 5 males (one non-speaking)

The action takes place in the lounge of the Mount Home for Retired Theatricals.

OLD ACTORS NEVER DIE...
ACT I

The scene is the communal lounge of the Mount Home for Retired
Theatricals. There are three high-backed armchairs upstage, with their backs
to the audience and facing a television cabinet and the large window. There
are net curtains at the window and elegant drapes. Downstage there is a
small sofa and two chairs around a coffee table. Stage left is a card table
against a wall, with a couple of chairs. Stage right is the door to the hallway.
The room suggests a large Victorian mansion and the décor looks expensive.
It is a well-run establishment for those with a comfortable income. As the
lights come up, REBECCA, JULES and PHYLLIDA are seated in the high
back armchairs but the audience cannot see them, so the room gives the
appearance of being empty.

ANN THOMPSON, the smartly dressed administrator enters, accompanied
by WALTER NEVILLE, a retired bit-part actor, who has a moustache, is
immaculately dressed with a military bearing.

ANN   ...and this is our communal lounge, Mr Neville. Not
everyone uses it – some of our residents prefer to watch
television, listen to the radio or read in their own rooms.
But I would say that most of them come here at some time
during the day. I'm sure I don't need to tell you that actors
are, in general, a very sociable lot.

WALTER   Indeed.

ANN   We always serve coffee in here after lunch and dinner and
residents can have other drinks brought to them here, if
they wish, rather than use the bar adjacent to the dining
room.

WALTER	How civilised.
ANN	Yes it is. We like to think that we run this establishment like a gracious country house hotel. We don't want our residents to feel as though they are in any kind of institution. We have disabled facilities for those who are infirm and all the staff, myself included, are trained nurses but applicants with serious medical needs are referred to our sister establishment in Surrey. So…you have now had the complete tour of the Mount Home for Retired Theatricals and, as I said to you when you first arrived, we do have a couple of places vacant at the moment. Have you made your mind up as to whether you will be joining us?
	(A voice comes from behind one of the chairs, followed by the other two.)
PHYL	Say yes, Walter!
BECCA	We'll never forgive you if you don't!
JULES	We need a fourth at bridge!
WALTER	*(beaming)* Am I on This Is Your Life?!
	(The ladies' heads pop up above the backs of the chairs and they are all laughing.)
ALL	Walter!
ANN	I presume that the three Mrs Sullivans do not need an introduction?
WALTER	No indeed, Mrs Thompson! These ladies have been my friends for over forty years!
PHYL	I was at drama school with Walter.
BECCA	I was at Chichester Rep with the old darling.

JULES	And I was in three films with him.
ANN	How lovely! It's always such a relief when new residents are welcomed with open arms. Oh, I'm sorry Mr Neville – I am rather jumping the gun in assuming that you will be joining us.
WALTER	Would tomorrow be too soon?
	(All three ladies squeal with delight and come out from behind their chairs, flinging their arms around WALTER and planting kisses on his cheeks.)
ANN	Tomorrow will be fine. You can have the room on the second floor if that is suitable.
PHYL	Oh good, you're on our floor – we can have midnight feasts!
ANN	*(in a warning tone of voice)* Now ladies…
PHYL	*(grinning)* Only joking, Ann. I swear.
ANN	*(not believing her)* Mmm. We don't have many rules here but the one about residents creeping about in the middle of the night to each others rooms is the one that we do enforce.
WALTER	Oh they're perfectly safe with me, I can assure you. I'm a confirmed bachelor.
BECCA	That's nineteen fifties' speak for gay.
WALTER	*(pulling a face)* Can't abide that term. Makes us all sound like pansies.
JULES	Walter's old-style, you know. Made a career out of playing sergeant-majors and policemen.
ANN	Oh my God! I remember you now! Weren't you in that film

with Alec Guinness?

WALTER   Yes, that's right! I was the sadistic company sergeant major.

ANN   Oh my mother had a huge thing for you.

WALTER   *(drily)* Sadly I wouldn't have had a huge thing for her but it's still nice to be appreciated.

(The MRS SULLIVANS titter like schoolgirls.)

ANN   Well, I'll leave you all to reminisce. I'm sure you have a lot to talk about. Shall I send Marcia in with some tea?

BECCA   Oh yes please.

JULES   And some of those Belgian biscuits?

ANN   Of course. And, Mr Neville – I do hope that you can exert a calming influence over these ladies. The Mrs Sullivans have been known to lead some of the other residents astray from time to time.

WALTER   *(smoothly)* Leave it to me dear lady.

(The MRS SULLIVANS look at the floor sheepishly. WALTER continues to smile as ANN exits. When the door is closed, PHYL puts her finger to her lips and opens the door to check that ANN is out of earshot.)

PHYL   She's gone.

(All four of them (including WALTER) explode into "teenage-girl" shrieking and then they link hands and dance around chanting.)

ALL   Ring A Ring a Roses

We've all got big noses

Big tits and big bums

And we're just great!

(They are supposed to collapse on the floor at the end of the chant but no-one can manage it and they all hobble off in different directions in pain.)

WALTER   Sorry darlings, I can't manage the tumble anymore. Dodgy back. Too much square bashing.

PHYL   Oh we're getting old! I've had two hip replacements. Becca's had knee surgery and Jules has got arthritis. Damn!

JULES   Oh never mind the aches and pains! Let's sit down and have a good chin wag. Come on!

(Everyone sits down round the coffee table and as they do, MARCIA appears with a tray of tea and biscuits. She is wearing a blue maid's outfit but without the cap.)

BECCA   Oh just in time! Bless you Marcey. We're all parched!

MARCIA   *(eagerly)*Aren't you going to introduce me to the new thespian? *(She produces an autograph book from her apron.)*

PHYL   Marcey, this is Walter Neville. Walter this is Marcey, an invaluable person that we cannot do without.

MARCIA   Oh I don't know about that! *(She holds out the book to WALTER)*

JULES   She wants your autograph Walter.

WALTER   *(smiling)* What me? You don't even know who I am dear.

MARCIA   *(reeling off all the information she has looked up)* Walter Eustace Neville, born 1941 in Swindon...

(WALTER stares at MARCIA in astonishment.)

BECCA	*(grimacing)* Swindon!
MARCIA	Attended Swindon Grammar School for Boys...
PHYL	Where he picked up some very nasty habits...
JULES	Not to mention several sixth formers down the local pub...
MARCIA	Then went to Cambridge University...
BECCA	Ah! The famous finishing school for confirmed bachelors...
MARCIA	And joined Coventry Rep for the 1963 season, where he played Laertes in Hamlet; The Fool in King Lear; and many other classical roles...
PHYL	It's the voice darling. You always had "the voice".
MARCIA	His first film role was in Tony Richardson's "The Charge of the Light Brigade"...
JULES	Enough Marcey! You can't possibly go through Walter's full list of film credits – we'd be here for three days! How many films have you been in darling?
WALTER	Two hundred and eleven.
PHYL	Good God!
WALTER	She's amazing! How does she do that?
BECCA	Marcey is totally stage struck. Every time a new resident arrives she goes on the Internet and memorises their complete resumé. It's awesome.
MARCIA	Can I have your autograph now, Mr Neville?
WALTER	With the greatest of pleasure.
	(He signs the book and a very happy MARCIA exits. PHYL starts pouring the tea and handing cups around.)
PHYL	Oh we're so glad you're here!

JULES	It's going to be great to have the old gang together again.
BECCA	We thought you were living in France.
WALTER	I was…but Martin died…
PHYL	Oh yes we heard. Poor you.
WALTER	And I didn't feel like staying there anymore. I wanted to come back to London but the thought of living alone in some flat just didn't appeal. But I got an email from my agent recommending this place, so I thought I'd give it the once over. I never thought I'd end up living in a home…
JULES	Oh no darling! You mustn't think of it like that! It isn't that sort of place at all!
PHYL	No, it really is like Ann Thompson said – a hotel for old…
BECCA	*(sternly)* Older …
PHYL	Sorry…older…actors. I mean most of us are still working – we can come and go as we please, within reason.
WALTER	You're still working?
PHYL	Yes! I'm doing voice-overs at the moment. Jules has just done an advert…
JULES	I'm the hip grandma in the incontinence pad commercials. It's ghastly really but the money's good.
PHYL	She gets mountains of free pads…
JULES	I don't need them you understand…
PHYL	No of course you don't darling! She gives them all to the office here, for the benefit of those who may need some discreet protection.
BECCA	And I've just finished a bit part in a West End musical!

WALTER	That's wonderful. But I thought this was a home for *retired* actors? Isn't that one of the rules?
JULES	Oh that's one of the rules that they never enforce!
BECCA	Yes. They'd much rather that we paid our bills, you see. So Ann positively encourages us all to keep working, if we can. But there's no compulsion.
WALTER	So, it really is like a hotel and not a home? There really aren't any rules??
PHYL	Well...
JULES	There are a couple. I mean the bit about going in each others rooms at night is a hard and fast rule but that doesn't bother us.
BECCA	God no! There are only four men in residence at the moment. One is gay, one is a perpetually grieving widower and two are over eighty, so there's fat chance of any nooky!
PHYL	And even if there was anyone decent available, one can always practice a bit of horizontal conversation during the day, if you get my drift. There's nothing in the rules about daytime.
WALTER	Er, quite. But you haven't told me why you're all here. I thought you were all sharing a flat in Knightsbridge paid for by your communal ex-husband?
BECCA	*(regretfully)* We were! And it was a lovely flat too! But we had to do everything ourselves! And it was so expensive!
JULES	Then Danny Stiller told us about this place. He came to tea one day and told us he'd moved in here and couldn't stop singing its praises...

WALTER	Danny is here?!
PHYL	Yes poor darling. He moved in the moment his wife died. Well you know she used to do everything for him. I mean she went on tour with him and cooked his meals... absolutely a slave to the man. Put the kids in boarding schools and everything.
WALTER	Is he still doing that amazing TV series. What was it? "The Master"?
BECCA	Oh God! *(She strikes a dramatic pose and voice.)* "The all-seeing, all-powerful Master of the Universe! He controls your mind and manipulates your desires". Load of old tosh! But incredibly popular. But no, Danny simply refused to carry on without Vanessa at his side. He just dwindled into a little sad mouse of a man. Mind you he's rolling in money. That programme sold all over the world and he gets fantastic repeat fees.
WALTER	I can't imagine Danny as a little sad mouse. I mean he *was* The Master – incredibly confident - almost egotistical in fact.
PHYL	Yes. None of us realised what an incredibly good actor he was. Apparently it was all down to Vanessa. She was the one who made him feel extremely self-confident. Once she passed away – The Master just evaporated. It's been three years now and he still hasn't got over it.
JULES	Anyway, because of Danny's recommendation, we came and had a look at this place and thought "This is for us!" Waited on hand and foot – no meals to prepare – beds made by other people – heaven! So we presented a united

front to our ex-monster and told him that he could sell the flat...

PHYL   On which he made a tidy profit, I can tell you...

JULES   And that from then on he could pay our fees here. He was quite amenable.

WALTER   Hmm. Wracked with guilt probably.

BECCA   Well, yes, there was that. We've always been able to play the guilt card with dear Edmund. It helped that he was shacked up with some twenty year old Bond girl at the time.

PHYL   Yes, and I'd just had my second hip operation, so Becca and Jules took me round there in a wheelchair.

WALTER   *(laughing)* I can just picture it! Was the Bond girl there at the time?

JULES   Sadly no. She was on location somewhere but we had cut a picture out of the newspaper of them together and Becca turned on the tears and did the "giving him the best years of our lives" bit.

WALTER   *(fondly)* You are such bitches.

PHYL   I know. But it hardly stretches one's acting abilities when dealing with Edmund.

WALTER   What is the old bastard doing now?

BECCA   Oh he's still in great demand – acting wise I mean. He's just been in the new Batman film and he's supposed to be in some film with Johnny Depp next year...

JULES   However, on the girlfriend front, we don't know. He's getting on a bit now, you know. He'll be seventy next year.

He doesn't go to the gym anymore and I don't think too many Bond girls have been beating a path to his door.

PHYL The last we heard – and that was about a year ago – he was dating some production assistant who was nearly fifty!

BECCA Yes, God! What a shock that was! I mean fifty! If he doesn't watch it he'll find himself reduced to snogging pensioners soon!

JULES Mind you, she looked quite a babe in the magazine we saw.

PHYL Yes but they all do now, don't they Jules? I mean look at Helen Mirren – in a bikini at sixty! But then they're all botoxed, surgically lifted and the pictures are airbrushed. Whereas our generation blew our good looks in the sixties and seventies, smoking pot and sleeping around.

JULES Speak for yourself dear!

PHYL Oh come off it, Jules! You slept with the entire cast of "Oh Calcutta" in 1971!

JULES Not the women.

PHYL I didn't mean the women…

JULES And we were all naked in that show…it was a huge temptation…

WALTER I saw that show twice. Once in 1969, when it first came out, and then in 1971 when you were in it. The two productions were markedly different.

BECCA How so?

WALTER All the men were circumcised in 1969 whereas they all seemed to be intact in 1971.

BECCA Fancy!

WALTER   I did. Quite a lot of them.

           (They all fall about laughing)

PHYL   Shut up you daft old sod! Oh it is good to have you back
           with us again!

JULES   Considering that you were maid of honour at *all* our
           weddings, it is only fitting that you should be reunited with
           us once more.

BECCA   Tell me...was that because you were our very good
           mate...or was it that you secretly fancied our husband?

WALTER   How could you ask such a thing?! Firstly, I knew and loved
           all of you before you ever became involved with the ghastly
           Edmund and, secondly, I have never fancied men who are
           in love with themselves.

BECCA/PHYL/

JULES   Oh how true/ that's Edmund/ you are so right... etc.

           *(DANNY enters. He is a timid man, with glasses, and his
           shoulders seem perpetually hunched over in misery.)*

PHYL   *(muttering)* Talk of the devil...*(louder)* Danny, love, you'll
           never guess who's our newest resident! It's Walter! Walter
           Neville!

           (WALTER gets up and strides across to shake hands.)

WALTER   Danny, old chap!

DANNY   Walter...is it really you?

           *(DANNY suddenly, to WALTER's ashtonishment, clasps
           WALTER round the waist in a hug and rests his head on
           WALTER's chest.)*

DANNY   *(on the verge of tears)* How wonderful to see you, dear
               Walter...

BECCA   *(whispering to the others)* Did we tell Wol not to mention
               Vanessa?

WALTER   I was so sorry to hear about Vanessa.

PHYL   *(muttering)* Too late.

DANNY   *(releasing WALTER, producing a handkerchief and
               dissolving into tears)* Oh my God...life is so empty without
               her....

JULES   *(getting up and going over to DANNY)* Now, now, Danny,
               come and sit down and pull yourself together. You'll only
               give yourself a headache again.

               *(She sits DANNY down and she and BECCA try to
               comfort him while he blubs incoherently.)*

PHYL   *(going up WALTER and hissing at him)* Nice one, Walter!

WALTER   *(looking helpless)* Well I didn't know what to say! You
               might have warned me! *(Lowering his voice)* I can't believe
               this is the same Danny I used to know and frequently
               despise because he was such an arrogant bastard. God he
               used to walk into a party and take it over! People used to
               groan when he arrived because the conversation would
               immediately be all about "The Master."

PHYL   I know, I know. Now he's just a shambling wreck of man.
               You know he sits in his room and watches DVDs of "The
               Master" every day. It's tragic.

WALTER   *(going over to DANNY)* Sorry to upset you, old chap. You
               mustn't mind me. I've spent too long playing sergeant

majors, you know. I've lost all sensitivity.

DANNY   *(blowing his nose loudly and making an effort to cheer up)*
             Not at all, Walter. It's my fault entirely. The girls will tell
             you. I just don't seem to be able to...get over...you know.

BECCA   Your loss.

DANNY   *(blubbing again)* Y..yes.

             (The women all exchanged exasperated glances.)

JULES   Did you go and see that therapist we recommended?

DANNY   Yes. But it just didn't work.

PHYL   Why? She was absolutely marvellous at getting all three of
             us through the menopause without anti-depressants. I
             absolutely swear by her.

DANNY   She was...*(groping for words)* too...nice. It just didn't work
             for me.

BECCA   But surely that's good isn't it? A nice warm, motherly
             woman to tell your troubles to?

DANNY   Y...you don't understand. Oh this is so difficult to
             explain...

JULES   Well you don't have to Danny. You don't have to explain
             anything to us. We're your friends.

DANNY   *(grateful)* Thank you darling. You're all my very good
             friends...the best friends anyone could have...*(he starts to
             crumple again.)*

PHYL   *(hastily)* Now Danny! You really must make an effort, love.
             Think of poor Walter! You'll frighten him away if you
             carry on like this!

DANNY   Oh yes. Sorry Walter. *(He puts on a very feeble smile and wipes his eyes.)* See...all better now.

BECCA   There's a good boy! Now, I think it's about time we
             repaired to the bar for a pre-dinner snifter, don't you?

WALTER   What a sensible idea!

             *(Suddenly MARCIA bursts in clutching a newspaper in a
             state of great excitement.)*

MARCIA   It's your husband! He's in the Daily Mail!

JULES   Really? What's he done now?

MARCIA   He's disappeared and Russian gangsters are after him!

EVERYONE   What!!!

MARCIA   It's all in here...look...look!

PHYL   Calm down Marcey – you'll have a heart attack or
             something.

JULES   Oh I haven't got my glasses. Can someone read it out?

             (WALTER takes the paper and starts to read.)

WALTER   The headline is "BATMAN ACTOR ON THE RUN".

BECCA   Oh my God!

WALTER   Sixty two year old Edmund Sullivan...

JULES   *(snorting with disgust)* And the rest!...

WALTER   ...who played the multi-millionaire villain in the last
             Batman Movie, disappeared from his London flat two days
             ago. This follows the mysterious disappearance, the week
             before, of his girlfriend, Tatiana Molinsky, the glamorous
             fifty four year old mother of Russian oligarch, Mike
             Molinsky. Neighbours in Edmund Sullivan's exclusive
             apartment block in Knightsbridge say that he was visited by

some of Molinsky's henchmen the night before his disappearance. A friend of Sullivan's, who was present in the flat when Molinsky's men arrived said, "They were very menacing. Big guys with attitude - and they made it very clear that they wanted to know what Edmund had done with Tatiana Molinsky. It was very frightening. It was like they were accusing him of her murder or something." The friend added that she was bundled out of the flat and told to keep her mouth shut. She took the next plane for Los Angeles and telephoned the London police from the safety of the United States.

MARCIA   Some friend! They could have shot Edmund the moment she left the flat! By the time she phoned the police they would have had time to ship his body back to Russia!

JULES   Now, Marcey, don't get carried away...

BECCA   Yes, the article specifically says that he was visited by these thugs the night *before* his disappearance, which would suggest to me that his neighbours saw him, alive, *after* the visit.

WALTER   *(patiently waiting)* There is more, if you'll allow me to read it.

PHYL   Sorry Wol. Carry on.

WALTER   The police issued a statement saying that Mr Sullivan was seen alive the next day but neighbours reported that he got into a taxi with a suitcase and appeared to be in a hurry.

BECCA   Told you.

WALTER   Mike Molinsky, who has long been suspected of organised crime activities, denied any involvement with Mr Sullivan.

He said that he had never even met him, although Sullivan has been escorting his mother for many months. He stated that he understood that some of his employees, who did know Mr Sullivan, had gone round to the actor's house for a friendly game of cards.

JULES   *(sarcastically)* Yeah, right.

WALTER   And furthermore, Mr Molinsky denied, categorically, that his mother was missing. "She has gone abroad for a holiday, that is all," he said but he refused to disclose her whereabouts. Police issued a further statement saying that they had no knowledge of Mrs Molinsky's alleged disappearance and her son had not reported any such event to the police. They are doing some preliminary investigation into the disappearance of Edmund Sullivan but until further evidence comes to light they cannot progress the matter further.

DANNY   Oh dear, what *has* he done?

PHYL   What has he done indeed? Even by Edmund's standards this is a frightening state of affairs.

BECCA   Oh, I don't know. It's probably on a par with the Las Vegas incident.

MARCIA   *(excitedly)* What happened in Las Vegas?

JULES   Edmund mistreated this girl in Las Vegas in the 1980s. Well, when I say "mistreated" it was really normal Edmund behaviour. He went out with her a couple of times, slept with her, and then dumped her for someone prettier. Only the girl happened to be the daughter of this big Italian crime lord who ran a couple of the casinos on the Strip.

PHYL   So Edmund was beaten up by a couple of Daddy's thugs
                and dumped in the middle of the Nevada desert in his Y-
                fronts.

WALTER   Yes, I would say that the Las Vegas incident would seem to
                be on a par with this latest one.

DANNY   All this terrible violence…it's bringing on one of my
                headaches.

MARCIA   Oh, poor Mr Stiller! I'll go and fetch your medication.

PHYL   Oh, Marcey… be a love and keep all this to yourself for the
                moment.

MARCIA   Of course! I won't breath a word. *(MARCIA exits, taking
                the tray of tea things with her.)*

WALTER   *(testily)* Oh get a grip man! Whatever happened to the days
                when you used to arm-wrestle stuntmen on film sets?

DANNY   *(getting his handkerchief out, his lip trembling)* That was in
                the days when I was a different person…when…my…

WALTER   *(even more irritable)* Yes! Yes! We get the message!

PHYL   There, there, Danny dear. Why don't you go to the bar and
                get us a round of brandies? We've all had a shock and we
                all need a drink.

DANNY   Yes, of course.

                *(DANNY exits. WALTER looks after him with some
                distaste.)*

WALTER   I have to say that Danny Stiller, the mouse, is even more
                irritating that Danny Stiller, the egomaniac.

PHYL   Oh never mind about Danny! What are we going to do
                about Edmund?

JULES	What do you mean "we"?
BECCA	And what do you mean "do"?
JULES	I mean, I'm sorry Phyl, but I wouldn't lift a finger to save my ex-husband if he was hanging by one hand from the side of the Grand Canyon!
BECCA	Me neither.
PHYL	*(sighing with exasperation)* You don't get it, do you? I'm not suggesting we help him out of any love, loyalty or for the sake of old times. I'm suggesting that we prevent anything from happening to the man who pays our sodding bills!
JULES	Oh.
BECCA	Right.
WALTER	Perhaps you'd be better off if Edmund was dead? Then you could collect on the insurance or benefit from his will?
	(There is a collective "Huh", "Fat chance", "Not very likely" response from the three women.)
PHYL	In the first place, none of us kept up the payments on whatever insurance policies we had on him...
JULES	I couldn't afford the premiums...
BECCA	Well he kept doing reckless things and they kept going up...
PHYL	And, in the second place, Edmund has never made a will. We know that because we all share the same solicitor and we've repeatedly asked him. Edmund won't make a will because he's been superstitious about it ever since Errol Flynn made one the day before he died.
BECCA	And even if he did make a will, there are three ex-wives

and two children to share...what? Edmund's debts? Because he spends money like water, you know.

JULES   Yes, we have to have our living accommodation fees extracted from his salaries at source. If we waited for him to pay the bills, after he'd lived the high life, we'd still be waiting.

WALTER   You said children – whose children? None of you have got any.

PHYL   No, of course not. There's the model in Brazil who bore him a child in 1973. That was the cause of my divorce from Edmund.

JULES   Then there's the child born to that French actress – whatshername...

BECCA   Dominique Badoit.

JULES   Yes. And that was the cause of my divorce from Edmund.

WALTER   You poor things! Why didn't you tell me?

PHYL   Pride...anger...whatever.

BECCA   I escaped that particular fate. If you remember, the cause of my divorce was when a drunken Edmund had a car crash in Monaco and the newspapers discovered he was registered into a hotel there, under an assumed name, with a young actress.

WALTER   What a litany of selfishness!

PHYL   Well – that's Edmund for you. Now, let's hope to God that the Russian Mafia haven't topped the old bastard before we can sort something out.

BECCA   Assuming we can find him – what can we possibly "sort out"?

PHYL	Well, we could get him to sign a will, for a start.
JULES	But he doesn't have any money.
PHYL	No, but he will have! Think of all those repeat fees! After he's dead and gone and we're all watching him in some bloody film on Sky One, we'll be coining it in.
	(JULES and BECCA realise the sense in this and they react with excitement.)
WALTER	You always were the clever one in our gang, Phyl.
PHYL	Thank you Walter. The only thing is, we're going to have to get a very good, watertight will drawn up by someone.
WALTER	My agent! Nigel is an absolute whizz at all the gobbledegook to do with copyright, repeat fess, residuals and whatever. I wouldn't be surprised if he's got a standard Last Will and Testament on file. I'll go and give him a ring now. Will Mrs Thompson let me use the phone in the office?
JULES	Of course she will. When you've finished, come into the dining room and have dinner with us.
WALTER	Is it allowed? I mean I'm not a resident yet.
PHYL	Of course it is, silly! We can have as many guests as we want! Anyway, don't forget – Edmund's paying for it.
WALTER	Oh well, in that case, I'll have a double brandy and whatever is the most expensive thing on the menu. *(WALTER exits.)*
BECCA	It's all very well drawing up a will, girls, but what if the Russians get to him first?
JULES	Well they didn't kill him the other night so, presumably, he

gave them a reason not to.

PHYL   Like what?

JULES   Well perhaps he told them that he knows where this
                Tatiana woman is and he's going to get her.

BECCA   Yes, that sounds like Edmund. He always talks his way out
                of tight situations. But what if he can't find this woman?
                What if he was lying, goes to ground somewhere and the
                Russians put out a contract on him?

PHYL   Becca, darling, you have to stop watching reruns of Spooks.
                Look, be realistic, where does Edmund always go when he
                gets into trouble?

BECCA
& JULES   (smiling) He comes to us!

PHYL   Exactly. So let's not waste our time thinking about Russian
                Mafia hit men and concentrate on preparing for Edmund's
                arrival.

BECCA   Let's go into dinner, I'm starving.

JULES   Good idea.

                (They exit but meet MARCIA in the doorway. She is
                carrying a newspaper.)

MARCIA   I've got the latest issue of "The Stage", do you want to take
                it into dinner with you?

BECCA   No darling. Leave it on the coffee table and we'll have a
                look when we have coffee.

MARCIA   Righto.

                (PHYL, BECCA and JULES exit. MARCIA goes over and
                puts the newspaper on the coffee table and tidies things up

a bit – plumps cushions etc .A man appears furtively in the doorway, but MARCIA has her back to him. He is wearing a black raincoat with the collar turned up, dark glasses, dark leather gloves and a dark trilby hat. He looks like an old-fashioned FBI agent. It is EDMUND attempting a disguise. He is also sporting a moustache like Hercule Poirot.)

EDMUND   *(speaking loudly, with a slightly dodgy French accent (think Inspector Clouseau) and making MARCIA jump)* Mrs Thompson?

MARCIA   Oh my God! You nearly gave me a heart attack! No I'm not Mrs Thompson. She's in the office, I expect. Do you have an appointment with her?

EDMUND   Um…I rang her earlier. She is expecting me.

MARCIA   Oh I'll go and get her then. May I have your name please?

EDMUND   Georges…*(frantically trying to remember)* …Fabergé.

MARCIA   Ooh, are you an actor?

EDMUND   But of course, mamselle. *(He bends over and kisses her hand.)*

MARCIA   Ooh, God! We've never had a foreign actor here before. I must go and look you up!

EDMUND   Huh?

MARCIA   I'll go and get Mrs Thompson. *(she exits saying dreamily "Georges Fabergé")*

              (EDMUND closes the door behind her, takes off his gloves and hat and paces up and down a little.)

EDMUND   *(to himself, without the foreign accent.)* I think the hand kissing might have been a little over the top. *(He goes and looks nervously out of the window.)* I don't think I've been followed but I'm not sure about that red car. *(He jumps back and gasps.)* Stay away from the window, you fool! It's in all the best scripts. Stay away from the window when you're being followed. *(He comes back into the centre of the room and sits down on one of the chairs around the coffee table.)* Ah, the good old Stage newspaper! *(He picks it up and starts to read.)* Only read by the great in spirit but poor in luck. Takes me back. Let's have a look at the ads. Actors wanted for the cast of Porgy and Bess – that lets me out…wrong colour. Actors wanted for drag revue – out again…wrong persuasion. Actresses wanted for a re-run of The Vagina Monologues – and it's strike three…wrong sex. Dear God, it must be bloody hard getting a foothold in the profession nowadays! When I was young there used to be loads of ads that said things like – handsome young men wanted for western film. Must be able to ride a horse and spit. Now they have to be able to snog another cowboy as well. Ah, life is so complicated…

(ANN THOMPSON enters, all smiles, and offers her hand. EDMUND drops the paper and jumps to his feet.)

ANN   You must be the French gentleman who telephoned me earlier. I'm sorry, I didn't catch your name.

EDMUND   *(resuming his accent, taking her hand and bowing over it but not kissing it.)* Georges Fabergé, madame.

ANN   And you are, of course, an actor?

EDMUND   But of course, madame…

ANN	Thompson…Ann Thompson.
EDMUND	Yes, Madame Thompson. I have been an actor for many, many years – both in France, Hollywood and here.
ANN	My goodness! I'm afraid I'm not much of a filmgoer, but might I have seen one of your films?
EDMUND	Er…I was in the Day of the Jackal…as a French policeman…er…several war films…er, most recently, I was in an episode of Poirot, as a Belgian policeman. There have been too many films for me to recount.
ANN	Of course. And what made you decide to come and live in our little establishment in England, rather than one in France?
EDMUND	But there are none in France, Madame! Actors are not respected in my country. *(He gets dramatic)* They are left to die…like old soldiers in the war of life…no respect….no work. C'est tragique, Madame. Only in England is the retired actor regarded with fondness and regard.
ANN	How awful for you. Well, I'm sure we can make you comfortable in your twilight years. *(EDMUND winces).* You're fortunate, as I said on the phone, that we do have one room left. Would you like to come with me now and I'll show you. Then I can take you on a tour of the place before you make your decision.
EDMUND	That would be magnifique, Madame. Please, lead the way.
ANN	All our residents are at dinner at the moment, otherwise I could introduce you to those who occupy the rooms adjacent to the one I'm going to show you now. But, if you would like to come in here after the tour, I'm sure several

	of them will be having coffee, and I can introduce you then.
EDMUND	*(panicking slightly)* Oh no, no…I wouldn't want to presume…
ANN	Nonsense! They're a very friendly lot. They love meeting new people. Now, if you'll just follow me… *(ANN exits, followed by an uncertain EDMUND).*
	(After a beat MARCIA enters with a tray of coffee and cups, which she places on the coffee table. At that moment JULES enters.)
MARCIA	Finished dinner already?
JULES	No. I've come to get my handbag. I've got some tissues in it. Danny's gone into a crying jag again.
MARCIA	Poor Mr Schiller! No-one would ever guess that he was once "The Master of the Universe". He's such a changed man.
JULES	Such a pain in the ass, more like. Who would have guessed he was such a good actor? Extraordinary.
MARCIA	Hey, there's a new bloke turned up this evening!
JULES	Oh?
MARCIA	Yes – a dreamy French actor called Georges Fabergé. I haven't had time to look him up yet but he's very distinguished. He kissed my hand and everything.
JULES	Ooh! Things could be looking up. Be rather nice to have someone with a bit of sex drive living here. French eh? Shame he's not Italian. I adore Italian men.
MARCIA	What are you like?! Do you know…I hope I'm still up for a bit of slap and tickle when I get to your age.

(MARCIA exits leaving JULES with a shocked expression on her face.)

JULES   *(to herself)* Thank you so much, Marcey dear. I'm not quite ready to go into flannel nighties and bedsocks yet. God, what a cheek! The minute you get to fifty they think it's all over. Well not for this chick, baby! *(She attempts to do a sexy walk to the door but it makes her hip hurt and she starts hobbling.)* God help us! I've got to get this hip seen to. *(JULES exits)*

(After a beat, a blubbing DANNY rushes in to the lounge and collapses into a chair. WALTER comes striding in.)

WALTER   Look, Danny old chap, I'm extremely sorry that I said the wrong thing. I had no idea that telling the story about your first film part would cause you to get in such a state.

DANNY   But you knew that we took our honeymoon at the same time as I was filming...*(he breaks off and clutches a handkerchief to his mouth).*

WALTER   You know, it's about time you got beyond this excessive grief. Have you sought help?

DANNY   *(nodding)* Yes. But nothing works. I've tried therapy, massage, reflexology, medication...I even went on a rebirthing course, but it set me back even further...

WALTER   *(sitting down and pouring two cups of coffee)* I do know what it's like, you know. To lose someone that you've been with for such a long time. Martin and I had been together for twenty three years. It's brutal when your closest friend and partner dies. I do know.

DANNY   Thank you Walter. I'm sorry I'm such a bore but, you see,

	it's more than that with me.
WALTER	How do you mean?
DANNY	Well, not many people realise…or they didn't when I was younger…that I'm not a very confident person.
WALTER	Oh, Danny that's not true! When you were younger you were *very* confident – to the point of extreme irritation, I have to say.
DANNY	No…but you see…that was just an act!
WALTER	*(surprised)* It was?
DANNY	Yes. Completely. I have always, all my life, been a shy, timid man who gives in easily to tears.
WALTER	Get away!
DANNY	It was only because of…Vanessa…*(he whimpers when he pronounces her name)* that I was able to function as a confident human being.
WALTER	But how? What did she do that helped you so much?
DANNY	Well, it's rather awkward for me to talk about. I've never told another living soul…but she used to …dominate me…you know…
WALTER	*(not realising what DANNY is saying)* What quiet little Vanessa? I can't imagine her dominating you!
DANNY	No…you don't understand…*(he looks uncomfortable and lowers his voice)* She catered to my special needs, Walter… eh? Understand?
WALTER	*(taking a few seconds to understand, as DANNY keeps nodding at him.)* Oh my God…oh ,you mean…ah…sorry old man…bit slow on the uptake.

DANNY   *(keeping his voice low)* I can't help it. It's been ever since public school. I have this…need…to be roughly treated by women…otherwise I can't be confident myself. I don't understand it. I just know that it worked.

WALTER   *(embarrassed but trying to be helpful)* Well, surely, there are…professional women…who offer that sort of thing?

DANNY   Yes. But I'm not confident enough to go to one.

WALTER   Mm. Bit if a Catch 22 situation there.

DANNY   I know. I went to the therapist that Phyl recommended but she was such a nice kind woman, it just made me worse. That's the problem you see. If women are gentle with me, it just makes me fall apart more.

WALTER   Yes. Unusual predicament. We'll have to get you out more. There must be some hard bitch out there who could sort you out.

DANNY   Oh I don't know. I haven't been out socially for a couple of years now – except to Phyl, Becca and Jules' flat when they were sharing. I've got myself so low now that I don't know how I'm going to get out of it.

WALTER   And I suppose that every woman that you meet expects you to be "Master of the Universe"?

DANNY   Exactly. You have no idea how much that series blighted my life. So many women were obsessed with the all-powerful Master, who treated women like playthings. They used to throw themselves at me all the time. I know you wouldn't think of it when you look at me now.

WALTER   No.

DANNY   It's an insoluble problem, Walter.

WALTER   I wish I could help.

DANNY   Well. It's been a bit of a help...being able to talk, as it were.

                (PHYL, JULES AND BECCA enter.)

PHYL   Oh there you are! You've missed dessert. There was crème brulee on offer as well.

DANNY   Oh. I think I might go and see if they've got one left. I feel quite hungry now.

JULES   Yes. You do that dear. It might make you perk up.

                (DANNY exits. The women sit down and start pouring coffees.)

BECCA   I don't know what we're going to do with him, really I don't.

PHYL   Did you have a good talk with him, Wol?

WALTER   Yes I did – and I know what the problem is.

BECCA   Oh do tell!

WALTER   *(Lowering his voice and leaning forward, so they all lean forward in a conspiratorial huddle.)* He's a masochist.

PHYL   Well that's a bit of a generalisation.

WALTER   No I'm not being general, I'm being specific. Danny is a masochist.

JULES   You mean Vanessa was...?

WALTER   A dominatrix.

                (All the women go "ah" as they understand, which then turns to distaste and they go "ugh!")

PHYL   To think she used to bake us all scones when we were in rep. I shudder to think what those hands had done.

BECCA	I'm sorry, I just don't get it. How bizarre.
JULES	I wish I'd known. I'm rather handy with a whip.
PHYL	Oh do shut up Jules!
WALTER	But listen, girls, he told me that in confidence. You mustn't breathe a word. He'd be mortified if you knew.
PHYL	Quite. But I shall never look at him in the same way again.

(DANNY comes back, eating a crème brulee from a little pot.)

DANNY	This is so good.

(Everyone just looks at him.)

What?

BECCA	Nothing at all, darling. Come and sit next to me and have a coffee.
JULES	By the way, gang. Marcey told me that we have yet another new resident. A French actor called Georges Fabergé.
PHYL	Oh French! How exotic!
BECCA	I do hope he's red-blooded. No offence Walter.
WALTER	None taken.
JULES	Well, Marcey said he kissed her hand.
PHYL	A hand-kisser! How divine!

(The door opens an little and the voice of ANN THOMPSON is heard Everyone cranes to listen and the women make various faces of approval at each other.)

ANN	*(offstage)* So, that's the full tour, Monsieur Faberge. Can I take it then that you will be taking our last vacant room?

EDMUND   *(offstage, still with his "French" accent.)* But of course, Madame. It is so charming here. I shall move in immediately.

ANN   Immediately?

EDMUND   But yes. I have but one small suitcase outside. My other possessions are in storage. If, that is, you do not mind my moving in immediately?

ANN   No, no! I shall get Marcia to make up the bed and do a quick dust around. If you would like to bring your luggage into the lounge, I will let you know when the room is ready.

EDMUND   But of course, Madame.

                  (ANN THOMPSON sticks her head around the door.)

ANN   Just to let you know that we have another new resident coming tonight. A French actor called Georges Fabergé. Can't stop, I've got to get his room ready.

PHYL   Righto!

                  (ANN leaves and closes the door. There is general excitement amongst the ladies)

JULES   Does my hair look alright?

BECCA   Fabulous darling. Pinch your cheeks and get a bit of colour in your face.

PHYL   Where's my lipstick? *(She rummages in her handbag, finds lipstick and a mirror and proceeds to apply it.)*

DANNY   All this fuss over a Frenchman!

JULES   I agree. I prefer Italians myself. Now if she had said that Franco Nero was moving in up the hall from me, I'd have a pair of fishnet tights on faster than you could say "lasagne".

BECCA
No offence, Danny, but it's been a very long time since we had any man in this establishment who had anything approaching a libido.

(The door opens – they all turn expectantly. EDMUND removes his sunglasses and speaks.)

EDMUND
(without an accent) Well if it isn't the Witches of Eastwick!

(There is a general groan of disappointment from the group.)

PHYL
Edmund! I might have known.

JULES
I suppose you're the mysterious Georges Fabergé?

BECCA
Of course he is. We should have guessed from the atrocious accent.

EDMUND
I'll ignore the jibe. Oh, and look, it's Walk on Wally and the Former Master of the Universe! How are you chaps?

WALTER
I do wish you wouldn't persist with that ridiculous nickname.

PHYL
Yes, Edmund. "Walk on Wally"! How can you be so insensitive?

JULES
Not to mention inaccurate.

BECCA
Walter has probably had more lines to say in the whole of his career than any of us put together.

EDMUND
True. It's just that they're always the same lines. *(He imitates a policeman bending his knees.)* "Hello, hello, hello" being one of them and *(He raises his voice to a Sergeant Major's shout)* "What do you think you're doing you horrible little soldier?!" being the other one.

WALTER   *(stung)* It's true that I have been typecast a great deal during my career, nevertheless, that does not make me any less successful.

EDMUND   No, of course not, old man. Just a bit of fun. Shake my hand and we'll start again.

              (WALTER rises and reluctantly shakes EDMUND's hand.)

              Despite my ill-chosen banter, I am glad to see you Walter. It's been a long time.

WALTER   Yes. Not since your last wedding.

EDMUND   Ah yes! The darling wives. Number one *(he plants a kiss on PHYL'S cheek)* Number two *(he kisses JULES' cheek)* and last but not least Number three *(he kisses BECCA'S cheek)*. And Danny old boy!

              (DANNY stands and shakes EDMUND's hand.)

              How's it going? Raking it in with all those foreign sales eh?

DANNY   Well, yes, I suppose so. Master of the Universe is apparently very popular in Russia.

EDMUND   *(shuddering)* Don't mention Russia, old boy. You may be popular with the Ruskies, but at the moment I am most definitely not.

PHYL   Yes we heard. It's been on the news and in the papers. You, apparently, have disappeared without trace.

JULES   Shame it's not true.

EDMUND   Well, I'm afraid it's going to have to stay that way for a little while. Just until this little misunderstanding blows over.

BECCA   Exactly what little misunderstanding is that?

EDMUND   Well...I don't want to bore you with the details...

PHYL   Oh please do! We're dying to know what's happened to Tatiana.

EDMUND   Ah. You know about Tatiana then?

WALTER   How could we not? It's all over the papers. You and the mother of a Russian gangster. Very colourful.

DANNY   So where is this woman?

JULES   Yes, Edmund, what have you done with her?

EDMUND   Nothing, absolutely nothing. I am innocent of her fate.

PHYL   Oh no you're not. You are never innocent of anything. Give us the full story.

BECCA   Yes – the full story.

EDMUND   *(pacing up and down)* Oh very well. I can see you won't be satisfied until you've wormed it out of me.

PHYL   No, we won't.

EDMUND   Well, I met Tatiana Molinsky at the premiere of the Batman film a couple of months ago. Very attractive woman. Magnificent body for her age...

JULES   Yes, thank you, we get the picture...

EDMUND   Well you wanted to know!

PHYL   Just get on with it.

EDMUND   We got on like a house on fire, even though she was older than my usual girlfriends...

BECCA   Again with the age thing!

EDMUND   I can't help it, Becca. I'll admit that I am attracted to young things ...well, not too young, if you get my drift.

JULES	Yes. We know that you manage to stay this side of creepy, dear.
EDMUND	Thank you. So, anyway, Tatiana became my latest squeeze...
WALTER	Your what?
EDMUND	Sorry, Walter, that's LA speak for "girlfriend".
WALTER	Oh.
EDMUND	Where was I?
DANNY	Tatiana was your latest squeeze.
EDMUND	Oh yes. Thank you Danny. Well, it was fine for a while. Very passionate woman, as Russians are...
PHYL	You would have extensive experience of Russian women, of course.
EDMUND	Well...I've known a few. I can't say that I haven't. Anyway Tatiana was exceptionally passionate and very ...er...possessive. She would get unreasonably jealous if I so much as looked at another woman and that just became tiresome. So, I'm afraid I strayed...
	(All the women sigh and tut.)
JULES	Really! Someone should take you to a vet and have your bits cut off.
BECCA	Or put bromide in your tea.
PHYL	Disgraceful.
EDMUND	Do you want me to continue? Or are you too busy fantasising about having my bits cut off?
PHYL	Carry on.
EDMUND	*(glaring at them)* Well, as I said, I strayed – with this

twenty-something actress and Tatiana caught us.

WALTER   What – inflagrante as it were?

EDMUND   I'm afraid so. She was incandescent with rage. Threw a lot
of things, as I remember. Threatened to kill me? Yes, that
was in there too – as well as brandishing a knife at one
point. It was truly terrifying. Then she just went. Pouf! Out
of my life. No pleading phone calls, no pathetic letters,
nothing. She just disappeared. The next thing I knew was
that there were a load of very menacing Russians in my flat
threatening to do unspeakable things to me if I did not
produce their boss's mother.

DANNY   So how did you get out of that situation?

EDMUND   I told them that I thought I knew where she was and I
would go and persuade her to come home.

WALTER   And do you?

EDMUND   Haven't the faintest idea, old man. Hence the checking into
here in disguise. Couldn't think of anything else to do. I
told my agent I was disappearing for a few weeks until all
this blows over.

PHYL   Well, I should say that this is a fairly typical Edmund
Sullivan scenario, wouldn't you?

*(Everyone except EDMUND nods and murmurs
agreement. ANN THOMPSON appears in the doorway.)*

ANN   Monsieur Fabergé, your room is ready now! If you'd like to
come with me to the office and sign the tenancy agreement,
then you can go and unpack.

EDMUND   *(Resuming his accent and bowing)* But of course, Madame.

Lead the way. *(He follows ANN, turning around at the doorway to speak to the others without an accent.)* I'm relying on all of you to keep my secret.

PHYL   Don't worry, Edmund, we wouldn't dream of letting any harm come to you.

(EDMUND exits.)

(grimly) Not yet, anyway.

DANNY   All this excitement has brought a headache on. I think I shall go to bed now.

BECCA   Yes, you do that dear. Have a good night's sleep.

(DANNY exits.)

WALTER   Well, I must go and get my stuff together. I'll drop off at Nigel's on my way here in the morning and pick up that will.

PHYL   Oh he's got one then?

WALTER   Yes, I knew he would. I asked him to insert a clause about repeat fees etc. passing to three ex-wives upon death. He was a bit confused for a moment, because he thought the will was for me!

JULES   Well done Walter. We'll see you in the morning then?

WALTER   Bright and early. *(WALTER kisses each one on the cheek, they murmur goodbyes, and he exits.)*

PHYL   What would we do without Walter?

BECCA   Yes. He's such a rock.

(MARCIA enters in a flap.)

MARCIA   There's a foreign reporter in the hall. He wants to speak to the three of you!

JULES   What all of us?

MARCIA   Yes. He's brought a photographer along and I don't like the
               look of him at all!

PHYL   Well, you'd better show them in, Marcey dear. *(To the
               others)* Thank God I put some lipstick on.

               (MARCIA exits.)

BECCA   I bet this is about Edmund. I bet all the newspapers have
               found out where we are and they're going to beat a path to
               our door.

PHYL   We'd better keep Edmund out of sight. Jules, go and warn
               him. Then come straight back. Having our picture in the
               papers might be good for our careers.

JULES   You never know. *(JULES exits.)*

BECCA   I'm going to enjoy this. We can be as nasty as we like about
               Edmund and he can't do anything about it.

PHYL   How true. There's always a silver lining in everything.

               *(MARCIA enters with MIKE MOLINSKY, an expensively
               dressed man in his thirties, and DMITRI, who is a large,
               menacing man wearing dark glasses. DMITRI never
               speaks.)*

MARCIA   Mr...er, sorry, what was your name again?

MIKE   *(he has a noticeable Russian accent)* Molinsky.

PHYL   *(under her breath)* Oh my God!

MIKE   And this is Dmitri – my photographer.

               (DMITRI stands with his arms folded and says nothing. He

just pulls a mobile phone out of his suit pocket and
displays it. This is supposed to be his camera.)

PHYL   *(nervously)* Pleased to meet you Mr Molinsky. Marcia,
could you come here a moment, please?
(MARCIA comes over, while PHYL scrabbles in her
handbag for pen and paper and dashes off a quick note.)

Could you give that to Jules please? And fetch some tea for
our guests? You would like some tea, wouldn't you, Mr
Molinsky?

MIKE   That would be very nice, yes.

(MARCIA exits, taking the tray of coffee and clutching the
note.)

PHYL   Please sit down. *(She motions to a chair and he sits.)*

BECCA   How can we help you, Mr Molinsky?

MIKE   I think we both know the answer to that, ladies. You know
that I am not a reporter. You know that I am the son of the
woman that your ex-husband has abducted.

PHYL   Oh not abducted, surely! I mean, we know that Edmund is
a rat but he's totally incapable of doing anything like that.

BECCA   Quite incapable.

MIKE   *(standing and pacing)* Your loyalty to your ex-husband is
touching. But ladies, believe me when I say that when I find
this pig of a man you once married, I will kill him. With
my bare hands. And perhaps a scalpel. *(He lifts up a*
sheathed scalpel from his top pocket.)

PHYL   Oh my God!

BECCA   Look, Mr Molinksy. We haven't got a clue where the pig of a man we once married is. If we knew, we would give him to you. Immediately. And probably sit and watch while you carved him up.

PHYL   Believe me, we have absolutely no loyalty to Edmund and we really don't know where he is.

MIKE   *(menacingly)* If you are lying to me…

            (He is interrupted by MARCIA bringing in a tray of tea things. When she has left, DMITRI closes the door and stands in front of it, with his arms crossed.)

PHYL   Look, Mr Molinsky, no-one is lying to you. Now sit down and have a cup of tea and let's talk this through.

            (There is a knock at the door.)

JULES   *(offstage)* It's Jules! Can I come in!

BECCA   It's the other Mrs Sullivan. She really should be here. Then we can all tell you our side of the story.

            (MIKE nods at DMITRI, who opens the door and lets JULES in.)

JULES   *(a bit flustered)* Thank you. Is everything all right?

PHYL   Perfectly dear. Mr Molinsky was just entertaining us with a description of what he's going to do with Edmund when he finds him.

JULES   *(cheerfully)* Oh something very painful, I hope?

MIKE   *(shaking his head)* This man must be very bad for you to hate him so much.

BECCA   Oh yes. Very bad.

PHYL   *(hastily)* But he still wouldn't have hurt your mother in any way. Edmund has never raised a finger to any of us.

JULES	He's never raised his voice either, come to that.
BECCA	No. Edmund doesn't do confrontation, you see. He never rows with women – he just ignores them.
PHYL	And tramples all over their feelings.
JULES	Breaks their hearts.
BECCA	Humiliates them.
PHYL	But he's a sweetie really.
	(MIKE gets up and goes over to DMITRI.)
PHYL	*(whispering to JULES)* Did you get hold of Walter?
JULES	*(whispering back)* Yes, he's on his way back.
MIKE	*(quietly to DMITRI)* These women appear to be mad. Is this place an insane asylum?
	(DMITRI shakes his head. MIKE goes back to his seat.)
MIKE	So, ladies, tell me how this man has broken your hearts?
PHYL	Well, I was married to him first. When I was twenty five and playing Ophelia to his Hamlet in Birmingham.
MIKE	Ophelia?
PHYL	Shakespeare. Edmund and I were Shakespearian actors at the time.
MIKE	Ah.
PHYL	We had a lovely big wedding in a church and a party in the theatre after the show. I found out later that Edmund slept with my bridesmaid during the interval...
MIKE	Interval?
PHYL	The twenty minute break in the middle of the play.

MIKE	*(appalled)* He slept with your bridesmaid on the day you were married?!
PHYL	Yes. But that was just one of many, I can assure you. He admitted, in the divorce court, to having had nineteen affairs during the course of our six year marriage and, then there was the child he fathered in Brazil...
MIKE	*(even more appalled)* Nineteen affairs and a bastard child?! *(slamming the table)* This man must die!
JULES	Wait until you hear *my* story! I was married to Edmund for seven years, during which he had seventeen affairs and fathered another child in Paris.
MIKE	*(beginning to have a grudging respect for EDMUND)* This man is some Casanova, eh?
BECCA	I suppose – although some would call him just immature. I mean his constant need for women is really all down to his constant need to be admired. And the fact that he has no morals. He sees nothing wrong at all in being a serial adulterer. To him, sex is just like having a conversation. A meaningless pleasantry.
PHYL	That is true, darling, so true.
MIKE	*(bitterly)* And this is the man who has despoiled my mother...
JULES	Oh despoiled! How wonderfully Shakespearian that word is!
PHYL	But highly inaccurate. I mean, with all due respect, Mr Molinsky, your mother is a little on the old side to be despoiled isn't she?
MIKE	My mother is fifty four. That is not old. Once upon a time

it was old but not now. Once upon a time, when Russian mothers reached fifty, they would become Matushkas - grow fat, wear black and crochet. Now, because of evil Western influences, they don't grow old *(his voice rises with anguish)* they take HRT! Suddenly, my mother is wearing the short skirts; dying her hair; having Botox injections... *(his voice drops to a horrified whisper)* Do you know what my mother asked me to buy her for Christmas?

(All three women shake their heads.)

New breasts!

(All three women tut and make noises of disgust.)

(MIKE is becoming unhinged.) My own mother, she says, Mikhail, I want my breasts uplifted – you can buy me the surgery for Christmas. What kind of mother asks her son for such a thing? My father has only been dead for eight years. SHE SHOULD BE GRIEVING! She should be wearing black, getting fat and...and...

PHYL   Crocheting?

MIKE   Yes! Doing the crochet! But instead, she is sleeping with this.....this...

BECCA   Pig of a man?

MIKE   Yes! This Casanova! This breaker of women's hearts! Other men have *real* Russian mothers *(he speaks with longing)* fat with white hair and blue veins on their legs – wrinkled stockings – who smell of bread and soup and keep their husbands warm in bed at night. *(He starts to cry melodramatically.)* I am cursed with a mother with the breasts of a twenty year old, who wears silk and furs and smells of Dior!

JULES   *(patting his hand)* There, there. It must be terrible for you.

BECCA   *(to PHYL)* Aren't Russians wonderfully dramatic?

PHYL   Wonderfully.

(MIKE suddenly stops crying and jumps up, looking murderous.)

MIKE   I have made up my mind. When I find this man who has abducted my mother – they shall both die.

PHYL   Isn't that a little extreme? I mean I can understand you wanting to take Edmund's life. God knows you wouldn't be the first... but your own *mother*?

MIKE   This is the penalty for having a sex-drive over the age of fifty. She should have thought of that before she shamed the Russian ideal of womanhood. *(MIKE strides over to DMITRI.)*

BECCA   *(quietly to the others)* He is quite mad, you know. You can see how the Russians managed to produce people like Ivan the Terrible and Stalin.

MIKE   *(quietly to DMITRI)* These women are quite mad, you know, you can see how the English managed to produce people like Prince Charles and Hugh Grant.

(Suddenly there is a knock at the door.)

MAN'S
VOICE   Now then, now then! What's all the commotion about in there? Open the door, there's a nice gentlemen, and I won't have to take you down the nick!

(MIKE nods at DMITRI, who opens the door and reveals

WALTER, standing with his hands behind his back, looking very officious. He flashes a fake warrant card) Detective Inspector Peabody, Westminster CID.

MIKE   Is there a problem officer?

WALTER   *(strolling confidently into the room)* You tell me, sonny. I received a report to the effect that you were intimidating these ladies and, furthermore, I understand that you posed as a newspaper reporter in order to gain entry. I'm afraid I'm going to have to take you down to the police station for questioning.

MIKE   *(smoothly)* There has been a misunderstanding constable...

WALTER   Inspector!

MIKE   I'm sorry – Inspector. We have just been taking tea with these dear ladies – is that not so?

WOMEN   Yes.

WALTER   Well, that's as maybe but I have to conduct an investigation. Ladies – if you would care to come to the office with me, we can talk about this matter in private. Gentlemen, I suggest you wait here until I have finished. I will want to take your statements.

MIKE   Of course, Serjeant.

WALTER   Come along ladies. *(WALTER ushers the three women out of the room.)*

MIKE   Stupid British policemen! Always interfering at the wrong time! Well, if he thinks we're waiting around here to give a statement, he's got another think coming. I know these women are lying. They are all still in love with this pig of

an ex-husband and they are protecting him. But I will find
out their secret…

(MARCIA bustles in to collect the tea tray.)

MARCIA   Ooh, hallo! Have you finished your interview then?

MIKE   Er…yes.

MARCIA   Are you an entertainment reporter? Only I'd love a job like
            that…you know…interviewing the stars. I'd be dead good
            at it as well, 'cos I know everything about everybody…

MIKE   *(getting interested)* Do you?

MARCIA   Oh yes. I spend hours on the internet looking up all the
            actor's biographies. Especially everyone who comes to live
            here. I'm dead good at research.

MIKE   Well how would you like to have a job on my newspaper?

MARCIA   Really?!

MIKE   Why don't you come with us now and meet the editor?

MARCIA   What right now? Oh no, I couldn't. I don't finish work
            until ten. I've got another two hours until my shift finishes.

MIKE   But supposing my editor could offer you a job straight
            away? They've been looking for someone.

MARCIA   Oh that would be a problem. Mrs Thompson would never
            find a replacement for me at such short notice. No, it's very
            kind of you – I mean I'd love the job and everything – but I
            couldn't let Mrs Thompson down.

MIKE   *(suddenly very menacing)* Oh, I think you could. In fact,
            I'm going to insist. Dmitri!

(MIKE snaps his fingers and DMITRI immediately grabs

MARCIA, covering her mouth so she can't scream.)

And please don't worry about a replacement, my dear. I have just the girl to take your place tomorrow. Meanwhile, you and I are going to have a little chat about all the people who come and go in this strange place. Dmitri! Take her to the car!

(DMITRI exits with the struggling MARCIA. MIKE smiles evilly to himself.)

OK, Mr Casanova, Mr Big-Shot actor who has abducted my mother – you'd better kiss your ass goodbye, because Mike Molinsky is coming after you and…*(his voice breaks with emotion)* and your Russian floozie of a girlfriend who has forgotten how to be a mother!

BLACKOUT.

END OF ACT ONE.

OLD ACTORS NEVER DIE...
ACT II SCENE I.

The resident's lounge, the next morning. WALTER is sitting reading a
newspaper. There is a large cabin trunk next to him (it is full of his
costumes), plus an assortment of cherished props such as swords, walking
sticks and rifles. PHYL enters.

PHYL   Hello darling. My goodness! What an assortment of
                weaponry!

WALTER   Yes, I know. Souvenirs of various films. I'm very attached
                to them.

PHYL   Of course you are dear. And you never know – given the
                current state of affairs – when they might come in handy! I
                didn't sleep a wink last night. Edmund, however, apparently
                slept like a log. Danny was complaining at breakfast this
                morning that he could hear him through the wall snoring
                loudly all night. Poor Danny!

WALTER   Well that doesn't surprise me. Idiots always sleep like
                babies.

PHYL   I don't suppose you slept much either. I mean you didn't
                leave here until past midnight. Such quick-thinking Wol.
                Wherever did you get the warrant card?

WALTER   I didn't, it was my Senior Railcard. If you flash it quick
                enough no-one notices.

PHYL   What a star you are! But you left so late, you must be
                exhausted.

WALTER   Well I wanted to make sure that the Russian gangster didn't come back. And you're right – I didn't sleep much. I was up at the crack of dawn and round at Nigel's flat for breakfast to pick up the will. *(He reaches into his jacket pocket and produces a brown envelope.)*

PHYL   Oh well done, darling! *(She takes the brown envelope and puts it in her handbag.)* Now we just have to figure out how to get Edmund to sign it. I'm sure an opportunity will present itself.

WALTER   Better get it done as soon as possible though. I reckon that Russian will be back again. He struck me as someone who didn't easily give up.

PHYL   No well psychopaths don't, do they? *(She shudders.)* All that stuff about his mother! Very unhealthy.

                    (JULES and BECCA enter.)

BECCA   Well that was the worst breakfast I've ever had in this place!

JULES   Absolutely!

PHYL   Yes, what was the matter this morning?

BECCA   Apparently Marcie called in sick and so everything was in chaos.

PHYL   Sick? She seemed perfectly fine last night.

JULES   I hate it when Marcie's not here. The place just seems to go to pot.

                    (ANN THOMPSON puts her head around the door.)

ANN   Sorry ladies about the breakfast. Marcie called in sick and it threw us a bit of a curve ball. But we should be fine today. Marcie, bless her, has arranged for her cousin to come in and cover for her. She'll be here in a minute.

JULES   What's wrong with Marcie? Did she say?

ANN   Some sickie bug, apparently. Her cousin said she was
             throwing up a lot. At least I think that's what she said. She
             has rather a strong accent.

PHYL   I didn't know Marcie had a foreign cousin. In fact I didn't
             know she had a cousin at all. She's never mentioned her.

ANN   I know. She's from Rumania or somewhere. We're lucky
             that she happened to be staying with Marcie this week,
             otherwise I would have had to get on to an agency and that
             usually takes forever. Anyway, I'll bring her in when she
             arrives. I hope you ladies will be patient with her today.

BECCA   Of course. We'll be lambs.

             *(ANN THOMPSON disappears. The women all look at
             each other.)*

PHYL   Are you thinking what I'm thinking?

JULES   Marcie doesn't have a cousin.

BECCA   If her cousin was staying with her this week she would have
             told us.

WALTER   *(worried)* You think the Russian has a hand in this?

PHYL   *(nodding)* Poor Marcie's probably been abducted. Oh God!
             I do hope they haven't harmed her!

BECCA   *(grimly)* If they have, then it's all Edmund's fault.

JULES   One more crime to lay at his feet.

WALTER   Do you think we should call the police?

PHYL   And say what? We think Marcie's been abducted by a
             Russian gangster who is looking for our ex-husband in

order to murder him? They'd think we were just batty old ladies who should be in a home for dementia sufferers.

WALTER   Well, we can't just sit here and do nothing!

JULES   Perhaps Mike Molinsky will offer to trade Marcie for Edmund?

BECCA   Yes! That's it! I bet that's the plan.

PHYL   Oh well, as far as I'm concerned, it's no contest. He can have Edmund in a heartbeat.

WALTER   Fine. But you have to get him to sign the will before you hand him over.

BECCA   Did you bring it?

PHYL   Yes, I've got it. We'll have to think of a way to get it signed this morning. There's no time to waste.

JULES   You do realise that we are standing here calmly talking about sending our ex-husband to his certain death at the hands of a Russian mobster?

BECCA   I know. It sort of makes life worthwhile – don't you think?

(Everyone, including WALTER, visibly brightens and murmurs "Absolutely", "Great", "Just what he deserves" etc. At that moment EDMUND and DANNY appear. DANNY looks worn out.)

EDMUND   *(full of enthusiasm)* …I can honestly say I've never slept in a more comfortable bed…I was out like a light!

DANNY   If only I could say the same thing. Have none of your legions of women told you that you snore louder than a rhinoceros?

EDMUND   What? Nonsense! I don't snore! That's ridiculous!

PHYL   Of course you do, Edmund. If I hadn't divorced you for adultery then I probably would have divorced you for the years of broken sleep.

EDMUND   Do I snore?

EVERYONE   Yes!

EDMUND   Well I never. *(Noticing WALTER's pile of weapons)* Good Lord Wally! Are you planning to defend this place against a Zulu attack?!

WALTER   Ah. Just some of my treasured mementoes from my films, you know. This one is actually from the film "Zulu". *(He holds up an ancient rifle.)* If you remember, I was a lance corporal in that film.

EDMUND   *(taking it and turning it over in his hands)* That's right! You had one line, I remember. It was something like *(he puts on a cockney accent)* "They're attacking again, Sarge...aagh!" *(He clutches his chest and staggers back as if shot.)*

WALTER   *(through gritted teeth)* I actually had quite a few lines in that film but, sadly, most of them ended up on the cutting room floor.

EDMUND   Never mind Wol. We can't all be stars.

(Everyone sighs in exasperation. ANN THOMPSON enters, followed by an unsmiling but glamorous woman of indeterminate age, who is dressed in a skin-tight nurse's outfit, which seems almost to have been sprayed on. Everyone gapes.)

ANN   Hello everyone! This is Irina, Marcie's cousin, who, luckily, is a trained nurse as well as everything else. She's going to be covering for Marcie until she's better.

EVERYONE   *("Hello", "Pleased to meet you" etc. Rather uncertainly.)*

IRINA   *(in a thick Russian accent – very grim-faced)* I will be doing whatever work is required. If you get sick, I will take care of you. *(She says it menacingly.)*

ANN   Let me do the introductions. This is Mrs Phylida Sullivan, Mrs Rebecca Sullivan and Mrs Jules Sullivan...they were all once married to the same man.

IRINA   You are Mormons?

PHYL   What?! Oh, no! We weren't married to him at the same time! I divorced him, then Jules married him, then she divorced him and then Becca married him and divorced him.

IRINA   And you are friends?

JULES   Oh yes! Shared experiences, you know.

WALTER   Or shared delusions, if you look at it another way.

BECCA   True.

ANN   Yes, well, this is one of our new residents, Mr Walter Neville.

(WALTER bows slightly and IRINA inclines her head in acknowledgement.)

And this is an even newer resident, a French gentleman called Mr George Faberge.

IRINA   Vous êtes français ? Je parle français couramment.

(There is an awkward silence as EDMUND doesn't speak a word of French. Everyone looks at him and there is an agonising pause.)

EDMUND	(hastily, in his French accent) Dear Mamselle, while I would love to converse with you in my native tongue, I feel that it is rude to do so in front of all these English people. You and I will have a private conversation later – shall we not?
	(Everyone is visibly relieved and IRINA nods.)
ANN	And, finally, this is Mr Danny Stiller.
	(DANNY, as if in a dream, comes forward and shakes IRINA's hand. She looks at him curiously.)
IRINA	This name – Stiller – I know it from somewhere. You were famous once – yes?
DANNY	Well...yes...
ANN	Er, Irina, I'm sorry to rush you but we have a lot of work to do. Mr Neville has just arrived and needs his room prepared.
IRINA	Of course.
WALTER	I'm afraid I shall need some help up the stair with this trunk, It's rather heavy.
IRINA	(marching forward and surveying the trunk) I will take it.
WALTER	Oh no, my dear...It's far too heavy for...
	(IRINA picks up the trunk, as though it were nothing and marches towards the door.)
IRINA	Please to follow me.
WALTER	Er...yes...of course.
	(IRINA leaves, followed by WALTER who scoops up all his weapons and exits. DANNY stands like a statue in the centre of the room, then he clasps his hands together and

speaks.)

DANNY	*(ecstatically)* She's so strong!
PHYL	Mm. I think if Marcie had a cousin who was a Russian weight lifter, we would have known.
JULES	This place is becoming like a madhouse.
BECCA	More like the set of "Carry on in Moscow" if you ask me.
DANNY	*(not listening to anyone)* I think I'll go and see if she wants any help.
	(He exits.)
EDMUND	What's got into him?
PHYL	I think he's rather smitten with Irina.
EDMUND	*(shuddering)* Oh my God! The very thought! I say that was a bit of a close shave when she started speaking French. I thought my number was up.
JULES	Quite. I should keep out of her way if I were you.
BECCA	She's obviously a spy for that Molinsky man.
EDMUND	*(worried)* Do you think so?
PHYL	Absolutely. And what is more, we think he's abducted dear Marcie and replaced her with that unspeakable woman. This is all your fault Edmund.
EDMUND	Yes, I know, I know.
JULES	Well, you'd better do something about it!
EDMUND	What *can* I do?
BECCA	You have to try and find this gangster's mother!
PHYL	Yes. Make some phone calls or something.

EDMUND	I wouldn't know where to start!
PHYL	Well think about all the conversations you ever had with the woman. Did she ever mention any favourite hotels, restaurants, nightclubs – that sort of thing? You could ring around those.
EDMUND	I don't know. We never talked much...
	(The women make various expressions of disgust.)
JULES	You really should be taken to a vet and have your bits done...
EDMUND	I beg your pardon?!
BECCA	It's not normal, at your age, to be so obsessed with sex.
EDMUND	*(insulted)* What do you mean "at my age"? I'll have you know that there are plenty of vigorous men "of my age". Getting older does not diminish one's capacity for lovemaking.
PHYL	Well it should. It's not normal. I wouldn't mind betting you've been taking something.
EDMUND	How dare you! I've never had to resort to artificial stimulants, I'll have you know.
JULES	Mm. We'll see. We're all going to accompany you to your room and supervise you while you make some phone calls...and we're also going to go through your bathroom cabinet and see what we can find.
EDMUND	*(protesting)* You'll do no such thing!
	(The women gather round him and begin to shepherd the unwilling EDMUND out of the room.)
PHYL	I think that's an excellent idea, Jules. *(to EDMUND)* It's

about time that women were protected from dirty old men
like you.

BECCA   You'll thank us one day.

EDMUND   Oh no I won't!

ALL   Oh yes you will!

               *(They drag him out of the door. There is a moment's pause
               and then IRINA enters, with a large duster, followed by an
               adoring DANNY.)*

IRINA   *(suspiciously)* Why do you keep following me?

DANNY   *(stammering)* I...I...just wondered if I could help you.

IRINA   I do not need any help. Go away.

DANNY   Oh please let me stay! I won't be any bother I promise!

IRINA   *(menacingly)* I warn you, silly little man, I will break your
               arms if you touch me.

DANNY   *(ecstatic)* Oh I bet you could too.

IRINA   *(looking at him curiously)* I feel I have seen you before
               somewhere, Mr Stiller. What did you do as an actor?

DANNY   *(slightly embarrassed)* I was in a long-running television
               series called "Master of the Universe." It was just a silly
               science- fiction thing...

IRINA   *(gasping with recognition)* Oh my God! You are the
               Master? Let me see...let me see... *(she drapes the duster
               around his head like a hood and covers his nose and
               mouth, so only his eyes are visible. Then she shrieks.)* Yes!
               You are The Master! I would know those evil eyes
               anywhere!

DANNY   *(pulling the duster off his head and looking embarrassed)*
Oh really?

IRINA   *(falling to her knees and clasping him round the waist)* You
are a God to me! As a girl in Russia I watched your show
every week. You were so masterful! So evil! If you had ever
come to Russia I would have given myself to you.

DANNY   *(surprised)* Good God!

IRINA   Say something to me, Master.

DANNY   I beg your pardon?

IRINA   Say something to me – like the Master used to.

*(There is an awkward pause. DANNY looks uncertain.
IRINA nods encouragingly, so he summons up the
character of The Master, places his hand on her head
forcefully and speaks in a powerful voice.)*

DANNY   You are my slave, woman! You will obey all my
commands! You will have no other Master but me!

*(IRINA shudders with delight and moans. DANNY beams
delightedly.)*

IRINA   Let me serve you, Master.

DANNY   Er...yes...well that would be nice.

IRINA   *(crossly, standing up)* No! No! No! You must be The
Master! I cannot give myself to a man who does not
dominate me!

DANNY   *(whispering hoarsely)* Oh I know exactly what you mean.

IRINA   Then do it! Be "The Master"!

DANNY   *(suddenly grabbing her by the throat)* Do not speak to The
Master like that, you worthless woman! Remember you are

my slave!

IRINA   *(delighted)* Yes! Yes! I am yours to command Master!

DANNY   *(lapsing into his normal hesitant voice)* So shall we..er...go upstairs?

IRINA   *(cross again and grabbing him by the throat this time)* I will only serve The Master – do you understand?

DANNY   *(almost choking but loving every minute of it)* Take your hands off me, slave, or I shall be forced to hurt you!

IRINA   *(grabbing his jacket lapels and dragging him towards the door)* Finally, the stupid actor gets the idea!

         (IRINA drags DANNY out of the room. There is a pause and WALTER backs into the room, having met IRINA and DANNY on the stairs. He is obviously shaken.)

WALTER   Dear God! That's not the sort of thing you expect to see in a retirement home!

         (ANN appears in the doorway.)

ANN   Mr Neville, have you seen Irina?

WALTER   Yes...I mean no! I mean I saw her in here a moment ago but she rushed out. I don't know where she is now.

ANN   *(sighing)* Oh dear. I fear she's not going to be a suitable replacement for Marcie. She's very odd, isn't she? Don't you find her peculiar?

WALTER   It's probably just because she's foreign. I'm sure she has her uses.

ANN   Mm. Perhaps you're right. If you see her, would you tell her I need her in the kitchen?

WALTER   Of course.

ANN	Thank you.
	(ANN leaves. WALTER sits down and then PHYL, BECCA and JULES enter. BECCA is clutching a bottle of pills.)
PHYL	I think it's absolutely disgraceful!
JULES	What was he thinking?
WALTER	Don't tell me you've met Danny and the lovely Irina as well?
BECCA	What? No dear. We're talking about Edmund and his human growth hormone pills.
WALTER	His what?!
PHYL	Yes. Can you believe it! The horny old goat has been taking human growth hormone pills for years. No wonder he's a menace to women!
BECCA	He claims he takes them for his backache.
WALTER	*(drily)* I think they've probably *given* him the backache.
PHYL	Disgusting! Anyway, what is this about Danny and Irina?
WALTER	Oh yes! I saw her dragging him up the stairs about five minutes ago. She was being very rough and he was smiling like a Cheshire Cat.
JULES	Oh! It's incredible! This place has gone from afternoon naps to orgies in the blink of an eye!
PHYL	This is all Edmund's fault.
BECCA	Of course. What isn't?
WALTER	Did you get him to sign the will?
JULES	No. He's constantly on his mobile phone at the moment,

ringing every hotel on the French Riveira trying to track down the mobster's mother. Every time we stick a piece of paper and a pen under his nose, he just waves it away.

PHYL   There has to be a way. We have to save poor Marcie.

WALTER   But even if you get Edmund to sign the will, how are you going to get in touch with Mike Molinsky to do a trade?

PHYL   Huh! I think that Irina can probably relay a message for us, don't you?

(Just then DANNY saunters in. He is a changed man. His whole demeanour is one of arrogant confidence now. Also, he has a red cheekbone and eye, as though someone has punched him.)

DANNY   What's that about Irina?

PHYL   Oh nothing, dear. We were just saying that Irina can tell Ann about our complaints over breakfast, that's all. What happened to your eye?

DANNY   *(smiling)* Oh that. I just walked into a door. Silly me.

WALTER   *(under his breath)* I think I feel nauseous.

(ANN puts her head around the door.)

ANN   I still haven't found Irina. Have any of you seen her?

DANNY   *(dismissively)* Oh she's making my bed. It got a little messy, so she's straightening it up.

ANN   Oh right. Well at least she's doing some work.

DANNY   *(winking at the women, who all look horrified)* Oh yes. She's been hard at it this morning.

ANN   OK.

(ANN disappears.)

PHYL	Danny! You haven't...I mean...you and...her?
DANNY	*(laughing)* Oh yes. I can safely say that The Master is back controlling the universe again.
WALTER	*(groaning)* Irritating though Danny Stiller the mouse was, I think I marginally preferred him to the *old* Danny Stiller.

(EDMUND comes rushing in, clutching his mobile phone.)

EDMUND	I've got a lead!
PHYL	Edmund, this is no time to be thinking about your career!
EDMUND	No, no! Not a leading part – a lead – a clue! It seems that Tatiana Molinsky stayed for a couple of nights in the Hotel Du Caprice in Cannes and then booked a ticket to Las Vegas!
WALTER	Las Vegas!?
BECCA	How did you get this information?
EDMUND	Oh the desk clerk at the Caprice often does little jobs for me.
JULES	I bet he does! The "smuggling girls up to your room" sort of jobs I expect.
EDMUND	Well, yes...I suppose so. Anyway, I shall now start to phone around the hotels in Las Vegas. I'm sure I shall track her down eventually.

(While EDMUND has been speaking, IRINA has appeared in the doorway, and has overheard what he has been saying.)

IRINA	Ah, Monsieur Faberge, it appears that you have lost your French accent.

EDMUND | *(thinking fast and lapsing back into the accent)* Ah, cher mamselle, you were impressed, no? I was demonstrating to my friends the quality of my English accent because I am going for an audition today.

IRINA | *(not taken in)* Really? Je pense que vous mentez à moi, Monsieur.

EDMUND | *(hastily)* Forgive me, mamselle, but I have some urgent business to attend to.

(EDMUND rushes out.)

PHYL | Wait a minute Ed...I mean Monsieur Faberge! We'll help you! Come on girls!

(The women also leave. DANNY and IRINA gaze at each other longingly and WALTER begins to feel uncomfortable.)

WALTER | *(clearing his throat)* Huh, hmm. Yes. Well if you'll excuse me, I must go and unpack.

(WALTER beats a hasty retreat. DANNY advances on IRINA.)

DANNY | *(He strokes her hair and then yanks it suddenly)* When are you going to be my slave again?

IRINA | Be patient, Master. I have to do some work, otherwise I will lose my job. Go upstairs and rest, then after lunch I will be your slave again.

DANNY | I shall be counting the minutes.

(DANNY lets her hair go and leaves the room. IRINA gets out a mobile phone and dials.)

IRINA   Tell Mike the man he wants is here.

           (She puts the mobile phone away and smiles grimly.)

BLACKOUT

END OF SCENE I

OLD ACTORS NEVER DIE...
ACT II SCENE II

The same room, after lunch. WALTER is sitting reading a paper and looking uncomfortable. He keeps clutching his stomach and is obviously suffering from indigestion. PHYL, JULES and BECCA enter.

PHYL	Oh there you are Wol! You missed dessert!
WALTER	I couldn't possibly have eaten it. Not after that main course.
JULES	Yes it was a bit grim wasn't it?
WALTER	Grim! They probably had better food in a Siberian Gulag! What was that ghastly thing she served up?
BECCA	What, you mean the stew that came after the cabbage soup?
WALTER	Stew? I thought it was someone's dirty washing!
PHYL	It was a fish stew. I must say it was rather reminiscent of the stuff that that landlady in Dundee used to serve us. Do you remember?
	(Everyone pulls faces and mutters "God yes!", "Ugh", "I remember that!")
JULES	Mrs McCloughlin. She was the worst cook in Britain.
WALTER	Well I think that title goes to Irina now.
	(IRINA enters with a tray of coffee and puts it down on the table, without smiling.)
IRINA	*(announcing)* Please do not require my attention for the next hour, I shall be busy.

(IRINA leaves.)

BECCA	We have to get Marcie back. I don't care what it costs. We can't put up with that woman any longer.
WALTER	I think you might get an argument from Danny about that.
PHYL	Oh for goodness sake! We can't put our digestions at risk for the sake of his masochistic tendencies!
JULES	True. Danny will just have to make other arrangements.
WALTER	Have you got that will signed yet?
PHYL	No. We have to do it this afternoon. It's a matter of urgency.

(ANN appears, dressed up in a smart hat and coat and pulling her gloves on.)

ANN	I'm out this afternoon, so I hope you will all be able to manage.
BECCA	You look very smart Ann! Going anywhere nice?
ANN	Yes, I am, as a matter of fact. Right out of the blue, I've been invited to tea at the Ritz!
PHYL	Oh? Anyone special?
ANN	No. Some magazine wants to do an article about Mount House and the journalist has invited me to tea to discuss it.
WALTER	What magazine would that be then?
ANN	Curiously enough, a magazine called "Russia Today". Why they should be interested in a retirement home for English actors is beyond me but I'm not about to pass up tea at the Ritz. Hopefully, they won't realise they've made a mistake until I've scoffed all the cakes! See you later!

(She leaves. They all look at each other.)

PHYL   I see the heavy hand of Mike Molinsky in this.

JULES   Absolutely. He's got Ann out of the way this afternoon and he's coming back for Edmund.

BECCA   Let's hope he brings Marcie with him.

WALTER   Better get Edmund to sign....

           (EDMUND arrives, clutching his mobile phone.)

EDMUND   Better get Edmund to sign what?

PHYL   Oh...er...our residency agreement, of course. It's up for renewal.

BECCA   Yes. It's an annual thing you know.

EDMUND   I don't remember signing such a thing before.

JULES   Oh Edmund! When do you ever remember anything mundane?

EDMUND   True. You'd better give it to me then. *(His phone rings.)* Oh, just a minute! This will be the Sands hotel phoning me back!

           (PHYL gets the will out of her handbag and carefully folds the document, so that the contents are not visible. She sticks it under EDMUND's nose.)

           Hallo Harry! Long time no speak eh? *(He waves PHYL and the piece of paper away.)* Not now, Phyl, I'm busy! Sorry, not you, Harry. So, any news for me? ...Uh,huh....OK....No. So she's not registered in your hotel, the Tropicana, or Circus Circus? OK. No, no, you've done enough. Thanks old man. I'll get on to Bud and see if he can work some of the other establishments. Thanks again.

How's the poker game going, by the way? You don't say? Fifty thousand dollars this time? It's getting too rich for my blood, Harry. I may have to give it a miss next time I'm in town! Take care. *(He finishes the call.)* That was Harry.

PHYL   Yes we gathered that.

EDMUND   Tatiana is not registered at the Sands, the Tropicana or Circus, Circus.

WALTER   We gathered that too.

EDMUND   So I shall have to call my friend Bud and get him to research the other hotels...

BECCA   Why do people on mobile phones think that their conversations are not heard by anyone else? Every time I take a train I end up knowing more about the personal lives of everyone in the carriage than I care to.

PHYL   Never mind about that. Edmund, just sign this agreement and then you can get on with your phone calls.

EDMUND   No, I can't do it now. I have to read it first.

JULES   Since when have you ever read things before you signed them?

EDMUND   Ever since I signed a merchandising contract for the Batman movie waiving my rights to a share of the profits from toys.

WALTER   Oh Edmund! What a stupid thing to do!

EDMUND   I know, I know. My New York agent had a heart attack. Literally. And, since then, I have sworn to read everything before I sign. No exceptions.

PHYL   Fine. We'll leave it until later then, when you're not busy. *(She quickly puts the will away.)*

EDMUND   Now…since you object to my phone calls so much, I shall take myself off to the dining room and continue my search for Tatiana. I can't do it in my room as there is the most God-awful row coming from next door.

WALTER   Danny's room? What sort of row?

EDMUND   It's like the soundtrack of a horror film – screams and the like. I saw him let that Irina woman in. Danny said she was going to give him a neck massage to get rid of his migraines. *(He shudders.)* My God, he must be insane. I wouldn't let that woman anywhere near me, if I were him.

JULES   Ah, but you're not him and Danny's…problems…have made him rather desperate.

EDMUND   Right. I'm off. I'm going to track down Tatiana Molinsky if it kills me. *(EDMUND exits.)*

WALTER   Which it probably will.

PHYL   Well, trust us to pick the one time in his life that Edmund chooses to be responsible about signing things. What are we going to do now?

WALTER   You'll think of something. Excuse me girls, I must go up to my room and get some indigestion tablets. If Irina is still here by tonight, I'm afraid I'm going to have to eat out. *(WALTER exits.)*

BECCA   Poor Walter. He thought he was coming to live in a peaceful and elegant retirement home, with lovely food and impeccable service. Ever since he moved in it's been chaos.

JULES   All thanks to Edmund, of course.

PHYL   I'm going to go into Ann's office and see if I can find some contract or something I can stick over this will. We have to get Edmund to sign it today. *(PHYL exits.)*

BECCA *(going over to the table)* I'd forgotten about the coffee. I think it's still warm. Do you fancy a cup, Jules?

JULES Might as well. Then I'd better get down to learning some lines for that audition tomorrow.

BECCA Ooh yes! Midsomer Murders isn't it? What part are you up for?

JULES Some eccentric old woman who gets murdered in the first five minutes. Pays well though.

BECCA Excellent.

(IRINA appears in the doorway.)

IRINA *(speaking over her shoulder)* Two of them are in here, boss. The other one is in the office.

(She steps to one side and MIKE MOLINSKY comes through the door, followed by his silent henchman, DMITRI. IRINA goes to fetch PHYL.)

MIKE Good afternoon ladies. We meet again.

JULES Oh God!

BECCA *(hastily)* We still don't know anything!

MIKE *(advancing on them menacingly)* But that is not true, is it? The woman who usually works here – the one who never stops talking – says there is a new man in this place, pretending to be a Frenchman. And Irina tells me that this new man, who is pretending to be a Frenchman, cannot actually speak French. I think, ladies, that you have been lying to me all along. And that makes me very angry.

JULES *(acting)* Oh please don't be angry! He threatened us if we

told you he was here!

BECCA   *(picking up on the cue)* Yes, yes. He's got a very violent temper! That's probably why your mother ran away!

MIKE   *(breaking down momentarily)* My mother! If he has harmed a hair of her head, I will kill him!

JULES   *(hopefully)* I thought you were going to kill him anyway?

MIKE   Yes. But it depends whether I kill him quickly or slowly.

BECCA   Can we watch?

JULES   Becca! I think that's a step too far!

BECCA   Yes. Sorry. Forgot myself.

(IRINA enters. She has PHYL in an arm lock and is propelling her towards the chair.)

PHYL   Ow! Ow! There's no need to be so rough!

IRINA   *(releasing PHYL, who rubs her arms and glares at IRINA)* This is the other one. What do you want me to do now, boss?

MIKE   Tie them all up. We'll see what a little unscheduled plastic surgery can do. *(He produces the scalpel and the three women shriek.)*

JULES   There's absolutely no need for that!

BECCA   We'll tell you everything you need to know.

PHYL   Yes, Edmund is here and masquerading as a French actor called Georges Faberge.

MIKE   Well, that didn't take much did it? Tie them up anyway. Where is the pig Edmund now?

JULES   In the dining room across the hall.

MIKE	Dmitri. Go and bring him here.
	(DMITRI nods and exits. IRINA produces a roll of duct tape, sits each woman in a dining chair and tapes up their hands behind them and tapes their ankles together.)
PHYL	*(to the others)* I feel a bit guilty about giving in so quickly.
JULES	What, risk being operated on by the gangster, just to save Edmund?
BECCA	I should cocoa.
	(DMITRI drags in a protesting EDMUND and throws him into an armchair, centre stage.)
MIKE	*(disbelieving)* This...is the man who has had so many affairs with women? Dmitri, close the door.
EDMUND	*(smirking)* Guilty as charged, I'm afraid.
MIKE	What is it that they see in you?
PHYL	*(sarcastically)* Huh! That's a question many of us would like answered!
EDMUND	Phyl, this is not a time for scoring points!
MIKE	*(being artificially friendly)* Tell me, truthfully, what is this gift you have for seduction? Is it because you charm them...?
EDMUND	Well a bit of that I suppose...
MIKE	Perhaps you whisper words of love to them...?
EDMUND	Oh, I'm sure there's a bit of that goes on...
MIKE	I'm sure that you flatter them – tell them they are beautiful, that they have wonderful bodies, lovely teeth, beautiful breasts...

EDMUND	*(smiling)* That sounds pretty accurate…
MIKE	*(turning nasty)* Or is it just that all these women are incredibly stupid!
BECCA	That sounds more like it!
MIKE	Like my mother! *(He falls to his knees in a tearful rage)* A woman who has lost her mind with grief over her dead husband…
EDMUND	When did he die?
PHYL	Eight years ago.
EDMUND	Oh. Hardly cold then.
MIKE	*(furious)* Do not mock my mother! Until she met you she was a good and virtuous Russian woman. Content to nag her only son about getting married and producing grandchildren. *(He buries his head in his hands)* Grandchildren that she will never see…
EDMUND	Why won't she see them?
MIKE	How can she see them if she is dead and buried?
EDMUND	*(shocked)* Who's killed her?
MIKE	*(getting nasty)* Don't play the Mister I Know Nothing with me! This is Mike Molinsky you're talking to. Head of the Russian Mafia in London. *(Getting his scalpel out and holding it to EDMUND's throat.)* Tell me what you've done with her, or I will slit your throat from ear to ear.
PHYL	*(closing her eyes)* Oh My God! I can't watch! Tell me when it's over!
JULES	Don't be silly, you'll miss the best bit!

EDMUND   I...I...haven't done anything with your mother!

MIKE   You're lying. *(He moves the scalpel to EDMUND's ear and takes his ear lobe inbetween his fingers and thumb.)* I am now going to cut off your ear lobe for telling me this lie...

                (BECCA screams and pretends to faint, then the door bursts open to reveal WALTER dressed as a soldier from the film "ZULU", complete with kilt and pith helmet, and with a Martini Henry rifle raised and pointed at MOLINSKY).

WALTER   *(in a military bawl)* It's alright Sergeant! I've got them covered! If they make a move I'll open fire!

MIKE   What the...? Dmitri!

                (DMITRI produces a modern automatic hand gun and points it at WALTER's head. WALTER concedes defeat and lets the rifle drop.)

MIKE   *(going up to WALTER and peering at him)* You! You are the same man who pretended to be a policeman yesterday! *(Getting angry.)* What do you think I am? Some sort of wet-behind-the-ears Boris, straight off the boat? You come in here, dressed in a skirt, waving a toy about and try to intimidate me?

WALTER   It's a kilt actually.

MIKE   What?

WALTER   The..um..skirt. It's a kilt, as worn by the Highland Fusiliers. A very fine regiment.

MIKE   Insane. You are all insane. Irina – tie this one up as well.

                (IRINA drags WALTER across to the corner. There are no

more chairs left so he has to be tied up whilst standing.)

PHYL   Never mind, Wol. You did your best.

EDMUND   That's the most lines he's ever spoken.

MIKE   *(whirling round to EDMUND)* You! Don't think I've forgotten about you! Now, where were we?

JULES   You were going to cut off his ear lobe, I think.

EDMUND   *(sarcastically)* Thank you, Jules, for reminding him.

JULES   Don't mention it.

                (MIKE takes up his position with EDMUND's earlobe again. DMITRI closes the door but then it bursts open, knocking him out of the way, to reveal DANNY dressed in a long black robe with a black, three-quarters face mask. It is his costume for The Master. He raises his arm dramatically.)

DANNY   *(in a loud masterful voice)* Who dares to disobey The Master?

MIKE   *(in disgust)* How many crazy people are there in this place?

                (He advances on DANNY with the scalpel.) This lunatic is going to be slashed open first!

                (IRINA screams and rushes over to fling herself in front of DANNY to protect him.)

IRINA   You cannot hurt The Master! He is all powerful!

MIKE   What?

IRINA   I have pledged my soul and my body to The Master. You will have to kill me first!

MIKE   Well that can be arranged!

(MIKE raises his arm to stab her. IRINA closes her eyes. Suddenly a mobile phone rings. MIKE roars with rage, turns into the room to find the offender, when he realises it's his own phone. He reaches into his pocket and answers it. DMITRI makes DANNY stand with the others.)

Mummy?

(There is an audible sigh of relief from everyone.)

Where are you?

EDMUND   *(to himself)* Las Vegas.

MIKE   Las Vegas? Why are you in Las Vegas? *(Pause.) (Horrified.)* You did what!? *(He roars with rage, hurls himself on the floor and has a carpet-biting tantrum.)*

PHYL   Whatever she did, he's not happy about it.

              (IRINA rushes over to him to console him.)

IRINA   Boss! Boss! Get a hold of yourself! It can't be that bad!

MIKE   It is. It's really, really bad. *(He bawls into a handkerchief.)*

WALTER   *(losing patience)* Well what is it man? We all want to know!

MIKE   *(pulling himself together but he can hardly bring himself to say it)* She's…married…a twenty five year old Mexican gardener!

PHYL   Oops!

BECCA   Overdone the HRT I think.

JULES   Lucky girl!

              (MIKE raises the phone to his ear.)

MIKE   *(mechanically)* Yes Mummy, I'm still here. *(Pause.)* *(Between clenched teeth.)*Yes, I will speak to my new Daddy.

(Everyone holds their breath.) Hello Enrique. *(Suddenly becoming venomous.)* Listen you Mexican gold-digging gigolo...my mother is a very sick woman...do you understand me? She may have the breasts of a twenty year old but she has the mind of a very deranged person. Did she tell you that her son is with the Russian Mafia? No? Well he is. And he is coming over to Las Vegas on the next plain to cut off your cohones – do you understand? You are a dead man! More than a dead man! And she is a dead woman! She is a disgrace to Russian womanhood! I will strangle her... *(he stops suddenly and his voice changes into submissiveness)* Hello Mummy. Yes, Enrique is very nice. I'm very happy for you. I'm coming over on the next plane to celebrate with you. Bye bye.

(He turns the phone off and screams at the heavens. Then he composes himself and speaks calmly to DMITRI and IRINA.)

Irina, book us on the next flight to Las Vegas. Dmitri, bring that stupid Marcie woman in from the car.

(He hands IRINA his mobile phone, which she takes, dials and walks out of the room with it clamped to her ear. DMITRI nods and leaves. MIKE turns to EDMUND.)
(menacingly) Now, what shall I do with you?

EDMUND   Now look here, Mike...can I call you Mike? I think you should be reasonable about this. As you are now fully aware, I did absolutely nothing to your mother – except annoy her. She's gone off and married this Mexican gardener on the rebound. It's not serious. I'm sure she can be persuaded to see the error of her ways and get a quickie divorce. They do them on every corner in Las Vegas, you know. And you could get the Mexican chappie deported or something. There's absolutely no need to go around killing people all the time. Especially me...

(DMITRI enters with MARCIA who is in mid-conversation, babbling away about nothing in particular.)

MARCIA   ...and so I said to her, there's no point in marrying someone like him, because he's just never going to get a job...he's a serial job loser...you should ditch him...

MIKE   *(interrupting testily)* Shut up!! My God, this woman never stops talking!

PHYL   Hello Marcie, are you alright?

JULES   We've been so worried...

BECCA   Life's been awful without you!

MARCIA   I'm fine! It's been a bit of adventure really. What about all of you? Everything alright?

            (They all look at each other in disbelief.)

WALTER   We would tell you the whole story, Marcie, but we're a bit tied up at the moment.

MARCIA   *(giggling)* Oh, so you are!

            (IRINA comes back, having finished on the phone. She hands it back to MIKE)

IRINA   OK Boss. You and Dmitri are booked on the next plane to Las Vegas. It leaves in two hours.

MIKE   I said book *all* of us.

            (IRINA goes to stand by DANNY.)

IRINA	I am not coming Boss. I am staying with the Master, who is going to keep me as his slave. *(Suspiciously to DANNY.)* You do have lots of money don't you? Enough to buy me furs and jewels and other things to make me happy?
DANNY	*(with a smile)* I'm loaded baby.
IRINA	Excellent.
MIKE	*(throwing up his hands in despair)* Fine! Stay with your old man. Dmitri! Come! *(To DMITRI)* What is it about women and old men!?

(The three Mrs Sullivans all say in unison "Money!")

MIKE	*(turning to EDMUND)* You are very lucky that I have other more important business to deal with, otherwise I would have cut off both your ears for messing with Mike Molinsky's mother.
EDMUND	Thank you, thank you. I promise that I shall never look at another Russian woman again…
PHYL	Or Italian. Remember that incident in Rome when that starlet's father tried to kill you?
JULES	Or American. Don't forget the Mob in Las Vegas.
BECCA	Oh and French. When you fathered that child, her brother threatened to kill you.
MIKE	*(disgusted)* You should go to a vet and have your bits done. Dmitri! We go!

(DMITRI and MIKE leave.)

EDMUND	*(annoyed)* Why does everyone want to have me neutered?
WALTER	It a natural reaction most people have upon meeting you.

BECCA	Hear, hear.
IRINA	*(to DANNY)* I am so excited by the sight of you dressed as the Master. I feel you need a massage.
DANNY	What a lovely idea!
	(IRINA and DANNY rush out.)
WALTER	*(shouting after them)* Oy! You could at least untie us first! Peasant!
PHYL	Never mind. Marcie's here. Marcie, do me first, there's something I want to talk to you about...
	(MARCIA produces a pair of scissors from her apron and goes over to PHYL to cut her free. PHYL starts whispering to her and MARCIA nods throughout. Then she cuts free the other women. PHYL pushes a piece of paper into MARCIA's hands. WALTER hops over to EDMUND.)
WALTER	I would love to think that you have learned some sort of lesson from this brush with death but I doubt it.
EDMUND	I'm beginning to think, actually, that I should go to therapy. When I look back over my life I can see that I have been somewhat fixated with the opposite sex.
JULES	Well that's a breakthrough and a half!
BECCA	Isn't it just!
PHYL	Edmund. Marcie is going to cut you free now and she is also going to ask you for your autograph – because she collects them. I do think that it is the least you can do.
	(MARCIA unties EDMUND and hands him the carefully folded piece of paper and a pen.)
EDMUND	Charmed, dear lady. Now how do you spell "Marcie".

MARCIA	Er...no. Don't put my name on it. Just your signature. Autographs are more valuable with just a signature.
EDMUND	Of course.

(He signs the piece of paper with a flourish. MARCIA holds it up triumphantly and all three MRS SULLIVANS punch the air in glee. ANN THOMPSON enters suddenly.)

ANN	The wretched reporter didn't turn up!
PHYL	Oh dear.
ANN	Still. It didn't matter. He sent a message saying he couldn't make it but that the tea was all paid for and I should stay and enjoy it. Which I did. It was a lovely, elegant afternoon.
JULES	Good for you.

(ANN notices WALTER, who is still tied up.)

ANN	What on earth...? *(Accusingly to the MRS SULLIVANS.)* What have you been up to ladies?
PHYL	Er...er...we were just having a little game of Bondage Poker.
JULES	*(catching on)* Yes! It's the reverse of Strip Poker. Instead of taking off an item of clothing when you lose a hand, you get tied up.
WALTER	*(also catching on.)* Yes! Thank you dear lady for interrupting us. I had already lost two hands. The next thing would have been a gag.
ANN	Good God! I'm not sure I approve of that, ladies. We can't have the elderly residents being tied up – no matter how innocently. The press would have a field day if they got hold

of it! I must insist that this game is never played again!

(Everyone agrees with murmurs of "No," "Absolutely" "What were we thinking" etc. ANN suddenly notices MARCIA.)

Marcie! You're back! Thank goodness! Are you alright?

MARCIA	Absolutely fine Mrs Thompson.
ANN	Where is your cousin?
MARCIA	Um...I'm not sure.
ANN	Well, I have to tell you, Marcie, that your cousin is not quite up to the job, I'm afraid, and I shall be glad to ask her to leave.
MARCIA	Oh that's alright, Mrs Thompson. I think she's got another job lined up anyway.
PHYL	*(as an aside to the other ladies)* Which pays considerably better.
ANN	Fine. Well I'd better get back to work and, Marcie, you'd better make a start on the dinner. Oh...but untie poor Mr Neville first.

(ANN exits and MARCIA unties WALTER.)

EDMUND	Do you know what? I'm rather taken with this place. I think I may take up residence full time...
EVERYONE	*(very loudly and with horror)* NO!!!

(BLACKOUT)

THE END.

FURNITURE LIST

Throughout: Three high-backed armchairs; a TV cabinet; a
                small sofa and two chairs around a coffee table; a
                card table *(folded up against the wall)*.
                Set dressing could be added, such as a vase of
                flowers on the TV cabinet, magazines etc.

PROPERTY LIST

NOTE : PHYL, BECCA and JULES should have handbags with them at all times *(except for page 30 for JULES)*

Page 5:   MARCIA brings in a tray of tea and biscuits; autograph book and pen in her apron.

Page 13:   DANNY produces a handkerchief from his pocket.

Page 15:   MARCIA appears with a copy of the Daily Mail.

Page 22:   MARCIA enters with a copy of The Stage.

Page 26:   MARCIA enters with a tray of coffee and cups. JULES enters to retrieve her handbag from which she produces tissues.

Page 27:   DANNY needs a handkerchief again.

Page 31:   DANNY enters eating crème brulee from a little pot.

Page 32:   PHYL rummages in her handbag for a lipstick and mirror.

Page 40:   DMITRI has a mobile phone in his pocket.

                 PHYL gets a pen and paper out of her handbag and gives MARCIA a note. MARCIA exits with the note and the tray of coffee things.

Page 41:   MARCIA enters with a tray of tea.

Page 46:   WALTER shows a railcard in a plastic wallet.

Page 49:   WALTER: large cabin trunk; swords, walking sticks and rifles. He is reading a newspaper.

Page 50:   WALTER produces the will in a brown envelope.

Page 55:   IRINA exits with the cabin trunk and WALTER exits with the weapons.

Page 58:   IRINA enters with a duster.

Page 61:   BECCA enters with a bottle of pills.

Page 63:   EDMUND enters with a mobile phone.

Page 64:   IRINA produces a mobile phone.

Page 66:   WALTER is reading a newspaper. IRINA enters with a tray of coffee.

Page 68:   EDMUND enters with a mobile phone. PHYL produces the will and a pen from her handbag.

Page 72:   MIKE produces a scalpel.

Page 73:   IRINA produces a roll of duct tape from her apron.

Page 75:   WALTER is carrying a rifle. DMITRI produces a handgun.

Page 77:   MIKE'S mobile phone rings. MIKE also needs a handkerchief.

Page 78:   IRINA exits with MIKE's mobile phone.
Page 79:   IRINA returns and gives the mobile phone back to MIKE.

Page 81:   MARCIA produces a pair of scissors from her apron.
                PHYL produces the will and hands it to MARCIA.
                MARCIA hands the will and a pen to EDMUND.

LIGHTING and EFFECTS PLOT

Start of play: *Music; lighting – interior-day.*

Page 48:   Cue: MIKE: "...girlfriend who has forgotten how to be a mother!"
Blackout, music, house lights, interval.

Page 49:   *Music, lighting, interior-day.*

Page 65:   Cue: IRINA: "Tell Mike the man he wants is here."
Short blackout, Music...which continues to...

Page 66:   *Lighting, interior-day.*

Page 76:   Cue: MIKE: "Well, that can be arranged!"
Mobile phone rings.

Page 83:   Cue: EVERYONE: "NO!"
Blackout, music, house lights, curtain calls.